The Centrality of Middle Class

Sociopolitical Resilience & Economic Stability

THE CENTRALITY OF MIDDLE CLASS

SOCIOPOLITICAL RESILIENCE & ECONOMIC STABILITY

DR. KHALID ALI AL-JUFAIRI

Hamad Bin Khalifa University Press
P.O. Box 5825
Doha, Qatar

www.hbkupress.com

All rights reserved.

No part of this publication may be reproduced or transmitted in any form or by any means, electronic or mechanical, including photocopying, recording, or any information storage or retrieval system, without prior permission in writing from the publishers.

No responsibility for loss caused to any individual or organization acting on or refraining from action as a result of the material in this publication can be accepted by HBKU Press or the author.

The opinions expressed in this book do not necessarily reflect the opinion of Hamad Bin Khalifa University Press.

First English edition in 2022
ISBN: 9789927161643

Printed in Doha-Qatar

Qatar National Library Cataloging-in-Publication (CIP)

Al-Jufairi, Khalid Ali, author.

 The centrality of middle class : sociopolitical resilience & economic stability / Dr. Khalid Ali Al-Jufairi. First English edition. - Doha, Qatar : Hamad Bin Khalifa University Press, 2022.

 120 pages ; 24 cm

ISBN 978-992-716-164-3

Includes bibliographical references (pages 109-119).

1. Middle class. 2. Social mobility. 3. Culture. 4. Social classes. 5. Economic development. II. Title.

HT684 .A65 2022
 305.55– dc 23   202228561387

DEDICATION

To **scholars** in the field whose
research focuses on the paradigm
of middle class and its discontents,

To **state institutions** whose works
are contingent on a stable
yet growing middle class, and

To **society** at large whose members
are an integral part in the course
of development and growth.

Contents

Acknowledgements 9
Abstract 11
    List of Figures 12
    List of Tables 12

Introduction 13
    Research Framework 17

Chapter 1: Class Theory: Social Stratification & Division 21
    The Theory of Social Classes 21
    Class Conflict 24
    Social (In)Equality 25
    Social Grouping: Societal Stratification 27

Chapter 2: Development Paths: Trajectories
of Sociopolitical & Economic Reforms 31
    Development is… 31
    Social Development: Advent of Economic Growth 31
    Limitations of Conventional Growth Models 33
    Human Development Index: A Tool to Measure
    Society's Advancement 35
    Achieving Growth, Stability & Continuity: Conditions & Terms 37
    Political Institutions & Interest Groups: Policy Formulation 38
    Rethinking Economic Growth: Sustainable Development 41
    Rethinking Economic Growth: Cultural Determinants 44
    The New Frontier is… 46

Chapter 3: Middle Class Engineering: Upward Social Mobility 49
    Social Structure 49
    Middle Class: Functionality 50
    New Middle Class 52
    Middle Class Endangered 54
    Middle Class: Economic Security 59
    Middle Class: its Unique Utility 60
    Middle Class: Today's Reality 61
    Sustainable Development: Empowered by a Growing Middle Class 62

Chapter 4: Post-Socialist, New Capitalist Serbia:
Middle Class Formation 65
    Post Socialism 65
    Serbia's Middle Class: Restrictive Social Mobility 67
    Serbia: Cultural Paradigms 70
    Socioeconomic Modernization:
    Post-Socialist Serbia 72

Chapter 5: Middle Class: Axis of Centrality 75
    Middle Class: Criticality 75
    Political Structure 76
    Middle Class: A Function of Growth 80
    Middle Class: Fostering Sustainable Development 81

Chapter 6: Entrepreneurship Exhibiting Socioeconomic Resilience 83
    Entrepreneurship: Social Modeling 83
    Entrepreneurship: Social Contextualization 85
    Community-Based Enterprises 86
    Entrepreneurship: Social Conditioning 87
    Entrepreneurship: Social Capital 88
    Social Entrepreneurship: Shortcomings 90
    The Business Model Spectrum Revisited 92
    Social Entrepreneurship: Rethinking 92

Chapter 7: Limitations: Rethinking Class Analysis –
Middle-Class Utility 93
    Rethinking 93
    Rethinking Middle Class Utility: Contemporary Research 93
    A Trend of Decline 95
    The Declining Number of Americans Self-Identified
        as Middle Class 96
    Rethinking Entrepreneurialism 97
    Social Mobility: Upward, Downward or Stagnant 98

Chapter 8: Considerations & Conclusions 101
    Social Classes: Societal Heterogeneity 101
    Societal Convictions: Cultural Determinants 102
    Culturally Contributory Factors: Empowering Sustainability 103
    Re-Engineering Middle Class: Sustainable Development Policies 105
    Socio-Culturality: Development Discourse 107

Bibliography 109

ACKNOWLEDGEMENTS

I owe immense gratitude to my greatest friends, Naser Ahmed Al-Suwaidi, Saleh Dawood Abdulrahman, Niki Leah Black and Ali Abdulrahman Al-Naama for their support and unconditional love.

To Naser, our friendship is joyful and eclectic as we weather life's storms with perseverance.

To Saleh, your constant support and care are forever embraced and cherished.

To Niki, we both bore witness to change, and that change is only the beginning of new – the world will be loving your voice.

To Ali, I am grateful for your friendship and advice throughout, especially as you are a fellow author and scholar in the field.

And to the rest of my friends, and to also my loving family and inspiring students, I am thankful for your immeasurable support and appreciation.

ABSRACT

Every country needs a growing and vibrant middle class, required for its economic development and its sociopolitical stability. The rise of the middle class has a multiplier effect – socially, politically and culturally, that a country should consider when creating its developmental path, vital to support the engine of growth. I argue that the middle class, as a social grouping existing within socioeconomic structures, possesses a complex and heterogeneous character, evident in developed economies from the time when the social division of society became necessary, and when the creation of a new socioeconomic structure appeared. The middle class primarily performs, social and economic functions, which endorse or criticize in-country policies. I further argue how the middle class acts as a socioeconomic guarantor of the progressive development in society, and how it also increases upward social mobility trend, encouraging the transition from one social layer to another. In the context of my book, I examine and build on how contemporary socioeconomic research references and employs the system of economic analysis of the position and role of the middle class within the stratification of society, matched against a key cross-cultural management (CCM) functionalist, dimensional paradigm of Geert Hofstede. I conclude that accounting for society's sub-social challenges and cultural determinants has a central utility toward devising development and growth.

KEYWORDS:

Middle Class
Social Mobility
Cultural Determinants
Social Class
Economic Development

LIST OF FIGURES

Wealth Gap between US Middle- and Upper-income households 55
Who is "Middle Income" and "Upper Income"? 56
US Middle-Class share within
the American National Income 57
Total Global Wealth Share: 2000-2014, by Region............................58
The Global Wealth Pyramid...59
Serbia in comparison with Vietnam 71
Rising Middle Classes in the Emerging Market Countries:
2000-2013..78
The Business Model Spectrum Revisited...91
The US Median Middle Class Wealth ranks 21 95
The Declining Number of Americans Self-Identified
as Middle Class..96

LIST OF TABLES

Only Upper-Income American Families Have
Made Wealth Gains in Recent Decades..55
Serbia's Economy: 2014-2019 68
Serbia's Economic Growth: 2014-2019 68

INTRODUCTION

"Thus it is manifest that the best political community is formed by citizens of the middle class, and that those states are likely to be well-administered, in which the middle class is large...where the middle class is large, there are least likely to be factions and dissension."

Aristotle 306 B.C.

Every country needs a growing and vibrant middle class, required for its economic development and its sociopolitical stability. The rise of the middle class has a multiplier effect – socially, politically and culturally, that a country should consider when creating its developmental path, vital to support the engine of growth. The middle class serves as a platform of upward social mobility, conducive to economic prosperity. Additionally, the middle class's development is linked to the strengthened in-country participatory structure: that is, countries characterized by large segments of middle class are likely to attain better administrative structures in which the population is not dominated by society's members from income extremities (Anthias, 2001). In the context of my book, I argue that the middle class, as a social grouping existing within socioeconomic structures, possesses a complex and heterogeneous character, evident in developed economies from the time when social division of society became necessary, and when the creation of a new socioeconomic structure appeared. The middle class primarily performs social and economic functions, which endorse or criticize in-country policies. The middle class, in itself, acts as a socioeconomic guarantor of the progressive development in society, and also increases upward social mobility trend, encouraging the transition from one social layer to another, while advocating for an economically viable, sustainable development.

I further argue that if permitting the wealthy to additionally amass public resources, the in-country poverty spectrum widens, depleting the socioeconomic structure, while increasing the rate of middle class decline. Hence, in-country development policies are to mirror a trajectory of social empowerment, which could very much yield societal resilience, provided proper access to resources and proactive policy implementation are both offered, namely sustainability-integrated economic outlook. As the growth of the middle class in society contributes to the in-country policy ability to develop its economy, economic growth associated with the middle class often involves cultural determinants, especially in middle class purchasing power and in its consumption of goods and services. Notwithstanding, Rodrick (2010) defines *middle class* as a category of social grouping whose percentile consumption ranges between 20 and 80 – the median per capita ranges at 0.75 and 1.25, yet cultural determinants of economic growth bearing a thriving middle class centralizes the socioeconomic necessity of class distribution. That is, as society's socio-cultural values may contribute or limit its ability to develop or cope with growth, I analyze and explain that those societal determinants classify and essentialize the discourse of development within the context of middle class growth while reconciling the trajectory of development to be sustainability-induced.

In Chapter 1, "Class Theory: Social Stratification & Division," I introduce and examine the continued utility of class theory as a central concept in the study of social inequality and class conflict in order to understand the dynamics and challenges of contemporary capitalist society. Social class and its class conflict have contributory socio-cultural relationships to define the factors of societal division.

In order to further analyze social division in association to social power and economic prowess, in Chapter 2, "Development Paths: Trajectories of Sociopolitical & Economic Reforms," I dislodge the assumed conditions of economic development and growth as societal gains and social development predispose economic growth, injecting into the analysis the Human Development Index factors for growth. As development trajectories are path dependent including sustainable development and its fiscal viability, in Chapter 3, "Middle Class Engineering: Upward Social Mobility," I analyze how the development of middle class is an integral factor for economic growth, and argue that devising the growth path and engineering the rise of middle class have a critical impact on social mobility, entrepreneurship, and innovation, especially within value-added industries. To deconstruct the analysis to include socio-cultural contributory factors of growth, in Chapter 4, "Post-Socialist, New Capitalist Serbia: Middle Class Formation," I examine Serbia as a case study of its middle class development, since Serbia's post-social transformation has created a new capitalist order suffering from cultural dissonance. In this case study, I overlay the analysis with Hofstede's six cultural dimensions, examining Serbia, comparatively, against a similar economic order of Vietnam.

As I continue in Chapter 5, "Middle Class: Axis of Centrality" to underline the centrality of middle class in a country's trajectory of development and socio-cultural gains, I expand on my analysis of the construct of middle class which is being devised as a source of social capital and as an engine of entrepreneurialism. In Chapter 6, "Entrepreneurship Exhibiting Socioeconomic Resilience," I further argue that entrepreneurship as a socioeconomic phenomenon fosters the conditions of development as a result of society's creativity, innovation and social capital – striking the right balance to create, or rather incubate, sustainable development. I analyze and explain how an entrepreneurial middle class can change conventional in-country growth models with limited economic freedom, lacking socio-cultural strengths in order to embark on a socially-driven, sustainability-integrated development. I conclude my book in Chapter 7, "Limitations: Rethinking Class Analysis – Middle-Class Utility" and in Chapter 8, "Considerations & Conclusions" by reconciling my analysis and recommending a new paradigm to rethink the utility and capacity of the middle class in sustainable development discourse and socioeconomic narratives.

To reiterate, the middle class plays a unique societal role, defined within economic independence/entrepreneurship and vertical social mobility, which characterizes a highly-valued, rewarding society. The latter becomes the mechanism in which the middle class can expand and thrive. Although the basic or rather the primary function of the middle class is social utility, societal stability is a function of the existing social structure in which the middle class ceases to exist. Thus, the middle class is a system 'stabilizer,' and once social structures are achieved, that middle class devises its grouping and positioning by exercising specific socioeconomic leverage. Additionally, and importantly, as culture defines the collective, societal, thinking process and the behavioral attitudes of society's members in a specific setting, if contextualized in the discourse of development, a society's culture determines the engageability of its members as well as the pace of development – economic growth and sustainability-integrated outlook. While recognizing the goals of sustainable development, society's culture, its social grouping and socioeconomic structure become hereafter paramount to achieving these goals. Hence, the middle class is aligned with the capacity building of sustainable development as the latter provides the social-grouping variation of the middle class with agency and voice – access to resources, disposable income, entrepreneurship and time-orientation adaptability.

RESEARCH FRAMEWORK

The comparative and relational study of culture in society or across countries has been on the scholarly agenda for a number of decades, as globalization takes on a new facet. Although the majority of empirical research is limited to the review of several countries, thus still not being able to provide a wider, yet nuanced picture – the choice of countries with different cultural settings and social classes puts forth variable assumptions on how the socio-cultural gap is modeled in society, hence analyzing the dynamics against or correlated to development and growth.

As the field of cross-cultural management (CCM) has gained significant intellectual and academic momentum, CCM hosts diverse paradigms and models, and in the context of my book, I examine and build on how contemporary socioeconomic research references and employs the system of economic analysis of the position and role of the middle class in the stratification of society matched against a key CCM functionalist, dimensional paradigm – that of Geert Hofstede. Under Hofstede's (1983) premise, society's members live in a social setting where they either self-mandate their actions or have to subordinate their interests as compared to the interest of the society at large, constituting its culture. National cultures differ from one country to another, although they are variably very stable over the course of time, in which the system of values remains in normalcy.

My book integrates the current body of knowledge examining middle class growth, its economic development, and also examining theories of social utility, sustainability, entrepreneurship and governance in class analysis by deconstructing correlations of political, social and economic realities. The primary methodology is based on all available indicators that distinguish the middle class from other social groups corrected against development trajectories including sustainable development, and I expand the analysis by integrating the socio-cultural nuances through deploying Hofstede's six cultural dimensions. The significance of Hofstede's (1994) cultural dimensions lies in its utility and ability to compare cultures across geographical boundaries, as the advent of the increasing social mobility from one cultural setting to another, which has significantly transformed culture in a variety of socioeconomic structures. In fact, this transformation has led to the change in 'cultural metaphors' across nations (Hofstede, 1980), as history, beliefs and norms are implicitly embodied within the diversity of social classes, in which the propensity of conflicts and of resolutions are heightened (Euwema, Wendt, & van Emmerik, 2007). I argue that employing Hofstede's cultural dimensions benefits the analysis of society's socio-cultural impact on development and growth, and these six cultural dimensions are defined and will be referred to, hereafter, as follows:

Power Distance

The concept of power distance is conceptually linked to the notion of "concentration of power" centralization. It indicates the extent to which society approves the uneven distribution of power in institutions and organizations. This notion is reflected in the values of society's members with little authority, and also in the ideals of those who are given much greater powers.

Uncertainty Avoidance

Uncertainty avoidance is associated with the structuring activities: formalization, specialization and standardization. The latter indicates society's lack of tolerance towards uncertainty and ambiguity. It is expressed in high levels of anxiety and releasing energy in a greater need for formal rules and absolute truths, and is less tolerated by people or groups of people with unconventional ideas or behaviors.

Individualism-Collectivism

Individualism implies a loosely coupled social structure in which society's members are assumed to care only about themselves and their families. *Collectivism* suggests that people can rely on care by relatives, clans, or labor organizations. More collectivist societies require greater emotional dependence of members from their institutions.

Masculinity-Femininity

In almost all societies, the predominant model of socializing gives men a more active role as converters of the world, while women have a more passive role as guardian of the family hearth. The range of data on the significance of goals pursued illustrates that for men, the most important goal is geared towards economic development and income growth; whereas for women, the improvement of quality of life and the betterment of society's relationships outweighs other objectives. Although many societies gravitate towards male-performance goals, transversal care and unity have increasingly gained momentum, reflected by the axis dimension of masculinity/femininity.

Time-Orientation

In a study carried out in collaboration with scientists from countries in South Asia, Hofstede and his colleagues identified a fifth dimension: *time-orientation* (Hofstede & Bond, 1988). In essence, this dimensional paradigm measures the perceptive difference of time between cultures of "short-term" and "long-term" orientation.

Indulgence – Restraint

Indulgence refers to a socio-cultural setting that allows the innate fulfillment of basic yet needed desires in society's members' lives, while *Restraint* strips society of its gratification, imposing regulative social norms as societal codes. An indulgent society believes that its members own control over their existence, as opposed to a restraint-induced society whose members assume external factors dictating their existence. In fact, this sixth dimension has a limited pool of data to correlate to its findings. However, *Indulgence-Restraint* encircles specific regions, namely the Middle East, given its sociopolitical animosity and cultural anxiety.

CHAPTER 1

Class Theory: Social Stratification & Division

THE THEORY OF SOCIAL CLASSES

Class is a large social group, with specific access to resources including wealth and power: the advent of socioeconomic stature. "Class" as a coined term of study was introduced within social sciences in the early 19th century, replacing "rank" – ranked and ranking, and "procedure" referenced to describe basic hierarchical groups in society. In fact, distributive rankings reflect changes in Western society's structure following the industrial and political revolutions of the late 18th century: feudal ranking began to lose its significance, and new, emerging social groups, including commercial and industrial capitalists along with a growing urban working class – had primarily been defined by economic terms, based on the ownership of capital, on the one hand, or the dependence of wages, on the other.

The application of "class" has become a central term in identifying and determining societal divisions of social grouping, based preliminarily on economic interest, stature, cultural positioning or origin. Anthias (2001) argues that "class as a mode of classification involves the allocation of individuals to positions on the basis of a range of criteria or markers: these may include work role or relations, skills..." (p. 847).

The origins of social classes as a theory can be found in the writings of sociopolitical philosophers: e.g., Thomas Hobbes, John Locke and Jean Jacques Rousseau, whose writings address key social issues and challenges of inequality pertinent to the 18th and 19th centuries. As Kiuranov (1982) argues, the knowledge of non-political public elements of the then-economic system and family kinship had largely determined the shape of political life in society. In fact, the latter was first introduced by the French social thinker Henri Saint-Simon, who had argued that the "state" form of government is consistent with the nature of the economic production system. The followership of Saint-Simon arose and entertained the theory of the proletariat, or the urban working class, as the main political force in modern society that became thereafter the cornerstone of the Marxist theory (Milios, 2000; Scott, 2002).

In an attempt to further expand the theory of social classes, beyond the confinement of its revision or proposition of alternatives, Bottero (2004) draws on Max Weber's theory and explains that the significance of social classes in the political development of modern societies is not as rightly understood as the Marxists claim; that is, its role in the societal process is played by religious, national and other factors. However, attitudes to class conflict, i.e., conflict and the struggle between classes for the right of control over the means of production, still divide social scientists and theorists involved in the analysis of class structure. Many opponents of Marx's theory have focused on the functional interdependence of the various classes and their harmonious cooperation (Milios, 2000). "Almost all theories of class begin from the assumption that the sphere of economic production is central to understanding the way in which material resources are allocated" (Breen & Rottman, 1995: 458).

There are three contemporary theories of social classes that explain the said phenomenon by examining social movements. The "New Class" theory assumes that these movements are related to middle-class interests, while the "New Social Movement" theory perceives these movements as a "defensive response to the encroachment of economics into other cultural spheres" (Rose, 1997: p. 464). The "Cultural Shift" theory proposes "that new social movements represent a change in values due to the growing wealth of society" (Rose, 1997: p. 464).

The political realities of the late 20th century show that in capitalist societies, classes lose their distinct character, and the antagonistic contradictions between classes weakened to a great extent that in most economically developed countries, they may not lead to serious political conflicts. Additionally, the prophecy of Marx's relatively successful revolutionary action of the proletariat against the bourgeoisie, and the replacement of the classless society capitalist system was generally inadequate, as evidenced by events in most socialist states throughout the 20th century and their full collapse for internal reasons between 1989 – 1991.

Sociologists often adhere to a common view on the characteristics of the main social classes in modern societies; defined largely by three classes: upper, lower and middle. The highest class in modern, industrial societies is composed primarily of representatives of the influential and wealthy dynasties. For instance, in the United States, more than 30% of the national wealth is concentrated in the hands of the 1% elite owners, providing a strengthened position, which does not depend on competition nor falling prices of securities. This 1% elite has the ability to influence economic policy and political decisions, which often helps to preserve and increase wealth.

The working class in industrial societies traditionally includes employees engaged in physical labor in the mining and manufacturing sectors, as well as those doing low-paid, unskilled, unorganized work in the service industry and retail trade (Inkeles, 2000; Camfield, 2004). There is a clear division of labor between skilled, semi-skilled and unskilled workers, reflecting a difference in pay and remuneration. In general, the working class is characterized by a lack of ownership and dependence on higher classes in relationship to its livelihood - wages. These conditions are connected by a relatively low standard of living, limited access to higher education and exclusion from areas of important decision-making.

Marsh (2003) points out that in the second half of the 20th century, there had been a general shift in the industrial economies from the manufacturing sector to the service sector, resulting in a reduced number of workers. In fact, the decline of the US and UK mining and manufacturing industries resulted in a permanent "core" of unemployment in which this layer of unemployed or underemployed workers is identified by a number of sociologists as the lower class, "objects." The middle class includes workers of mid- and senior-level engineers, academics, middle managers, and owners of small shops and businesses. The middle class merges with the upper class breeding wealthy corporate managers and executives, while the merger of middle and lower classes is often common in low-paid jobs of retail, distribution and transport industries.

The rise of living standards in Western industrial societies and changes in social policy, as manifested in the creation of a better social security system, has led to significant changes in the class system. Higher living standards, greater social mobility and income redistribution (taxes) contribute to the emergence of a large middle class, and tend to blur the differences between classes (Li, 2008; Berberoglu, 2007). These changes have generally influenced the declining popularity of class ideologies and the weakening of class conflicts. The middle class is envisaged as the supporting base of economic, political and social stability in the society.

CLASS CONFLICT

Berberoglu (1999) argues that "class conflicts and class struggles are manifestations of social and political divisions in society that are at base a reflection of relations of production" (p. 79). In fact, the well-known German-British sociologist and ideologist of liberal orientation, Dahrendorf (1959) claims that, in post-industrial society the basic contradiction of the social system moves the economic plane from the sphere of property relations to the zone of domination-subordination, and the main conflict, hereafter, is associated with the redistribution of power. Accordingly, Dahrendorf (1959) defines conflict as any relationship between elements, which can be characterized by objective or subjective opposites. The latter focuses on structural conflicts, which represent only one type of social conflicts.

The path from the steady state of social structure to the unfolding social conflicts, which means, as a rule, the formation of conflict groups, analytically takes place in three stages. The first phase is linked with the emergence of the causal background of latent, but actually opposite to each other, interests which represent two units of social positioning in the form of quasigroups. The second stage of the conflict is in the consciousness of latent interests and quasigroups in actual groups: i.e., interest groups. Conflicts always strive towards crystallization and articulation. For the manifestation of conflicts, certain conditions have to be met: technical (personal, ideological, material); social (systematic recruiting, communication); and political (freedom coalition). The third stage is to deploy the generated conflict – the clash between the parties, in a different distinct identity (nation, political organization, and so on) (Dahrendorf, 1959). Dahrendorf's theory premises that conflict leads to consensus, yet this consensus may be discrepant, creating inequality or dysfunctional building stratification.

SOCIAL (IN)EQUALITY

Can there exist a society without social inequality? The answer lies in understanding the causes of the unequal positioning of society's members. Sociology, as a discipline of study alone, lacks a single universal explanation for this phenomenon. There are varying methodological schools and theories that interpret social inequality differently. For example, social functionalism explains inequality based on the diverse social roles played by the different layers, classes, and communities. *Functioning*: the development of society is possible only through division of labor, where each social group provides a solution for the corresponding critical and integral path of the asked tasks – some members are engaged in the production of material goods, others create spiritual values, the third controls, etc. Essentially, a functioning society requires an optimal management of all kinds of human activity. As some tasks are deemed more important than others, the social hierarchy is invariably with those who provide overall direction and management of society. Only they can maintain and ensure social unity by creating the necessary conditions for the successful implementation of other functions.

The discourse of social inequality in the principal functionality is fraught with seriously dangerous subjectivist interpretation as both Marshall and Swift (1993) argue. However, why is one function considered more significant against another, if society as a whole cannot exist without functional diversity? The principle of functionality is limited in its approach, and does not engage in the societal existing realities as recognition for an individual belonging to the higher strata in the absence of its direct involvement in management. That is, as Talcott Parsons once pointed out, social hierarchy is a necessary factor in ensuring the viability of the social system, which is linked to the configuration system of dominant values within society. Marshall and Swift (1993) argue that Parsons' understanding of the location of social strata in a hierarchy is defined by society's formative views on the significance of each of its members. Nissel (1995) concurs and further argues that since every member occupying a certain place in society acquires its status, social inequality is, hence the inequality of status, resulting from the ability of individuals to perform a particular social role. That social role is thus observed to empower each society's members to reach a higher status.

In its specifically economic context, the root cause of social inequality lies within the unequal relation to the distribution of wealth and property – very much aligned with Marxism. Accordingly, the emergence of private property has led to social stratification, creating antagonistic classes. The exaggeration of private property's role in the social stratification of society has pushed Marx and his followers to the conclusion that the only possibility to eliminate social inequality would be by establishing public ownership of the means of production (Reay, 1998; Staples, Schwalbe, & Gecas, 1984).

The lack of a unified approach, describing and explaining the origins of social inequality is a reflection of how it is understood. Written history does not know of societies without social inequality. The struggle of people, parties, groups, and classes – it is a struggle for the possession of great social features, advantages and benefits. If inequality is an integral property of society, it has hence a positive function. Society reproduces inequality because it needs the latter as a source of sustenance and development.

Additionally, inequality is often referenced as the unequal relationship between society's members and social groups. Therefore, there is this tendency to identify the origins of these unequal provisions as situational-specific in society: in the ownership, power, and social qualities of its members. In fact, Crutchfield and Pettinicchio (2009) argue that "cultures of inequality - where many of the politically powerful or the electorate have a high taste for inequality - determine societies' response to social problems" (p. 136). Hence, any social institution or organization strives to preserve inequality, seen as marshalling the beginning, without the reproduction of social relations and integration of the 'new.' This is inherent within society as a whole.

SOCIAL GROUPING: SOCIETAL STRATIFICATION

As society evolves, its social groups develop invariably, ensuring access to the privileged and providing unequal distribution of social benefits. In other words, all societies throughout history have had a social dogma of inequality. The ancient philosopher Plato once argued that any city, no matter how small it was, is, in fact, divided into two halves – one for the poor, another for the rich, and those two halves quarrel among themselves. In essence, the unequal division of the two halves creates stratification. As a principal concept in sociology, social "stratification" derives from Latin "stratum" – a layer and "facio." As Chapman (1996) notes, the Italian economist and sociologist Vilfredo Pareto pointed out that social stratification, varying in form, existed in all societies. Similarly, the 20th-century sociologist Pitirim Sorokin argued that, in any society, at any time there is a constant struggle between the forces of stratification and the forces of alignment.

The term "stratification" came into sociology from geology, indicating the location of the Earth's strata on a vertical line. Social stratification, however, is understood to be a vertical slice of the location of society's members and social groups in horizontal layers – strata, based on principal factors including income inequality, access to education, the amount of power and influence, and professional prestige and stature. At its core, stratification is social differentiation – the emerging process of functionally specialized institutions, and also the division of labor. A highly developed society is characterized by a complex and differentiated device, diverse and rich status-role system. Guveli, Need, and de Graaf (2007) argue that social status is inevitable in society as its members continually seek out roles of power and tasks of exerting influence. However, social status does not inherently translate into differentiation, reflecting a hierarchical order, hereafter inequality. Guveli et al (2007) point out that age is an unqualifying factor for social inequality, yet affirm the varying social statuses as being different – e.g., a minor/child.

Although inequality has never ceased to exist in society, the interplay of social norms, beliefs, preferences and value orientation has amplified the degree of social inequality. Chakraborty (2002) notes that the origin of social inequality, its attitude and ways of its elimination, has always generated a lot of interest, not only from the thinkers and politicians, but also ordinary members of society who consider social inequality unfair. In the history of social thought, stratification is described within political discourse as the prime contributor to social inequality – divine providence, the imperfection of human nature, functional needs by analogy with the body. In fact, Karl Marx, in his eminent work, *The Communist Manifesto*, depicted social class struggle and inequality.

> "All previous historical movements were movements of minorities, or in the interest of minorities…The proletariat, the lowest stratum of our present society, cannot stir, cannot raise itself up, without the whole superincumbent strata of official society being sprung into the air." (Marx and Engels, p. 25, 2008)

Karl Marx linked social inequality with the advent of private property and the conflict of interests within different classes and social groups. Ralf Dahrendorf similarly argued that economic and social inequalities, underlying the ongoing conflict of groups and classes along with the struggle for the redistribution of power and status, is formed as a result of the market mechanism of supply and demand regulation (Dahrendorf, 1959; Parks & Vu, 1994). Pitirim Sorokin explained the inevitability of social inequality to key factors including internal bio-psychical differences between and among people; the environment (natural and social), objectively puts individuals at a disadvantage; collective life of individuals, which requires the development of attitudes and behaviors that lead to social stratification (Crutchfield & Pettinicchio, 2009; Slomczynski & Janicka, 2008). Therefore, social stratification translates into a hierarchy of social values, while social inequality is inevitable and reflects a historical process of societal development.

Notwithstanding, culturally-specific social inequality represents today's class stratification, and in attempt to address differences in a cross-cultural, industrial domain, Geert Hofstede conducted an extensive study of diverse cultures, identifying six key salient cultural dimensions: power distance, uncertainty avoidance, individualism-collectivism, masculinity-femininity, time orientation, and indulgence – restraint – kindly refer to my introduction chapter to read the definitions. He aimed to install these six national culture dimensions to address specific socially-culture and culturally-social challenges. However, Anthias (2001) claims that "social divisions are neither permanent nor fixed given social constructions" (p. 844). The problem of social inequality is one of the most acute and urgent in the modern world. A feature of society's social structure is a strong social polarization – dividing the population into rich and poor in the absence of a substantial middle layer, acting as a basis of economically stable and developed state (Mondale & Canache, 2004). Strong social stratification characterizes today's society, reproducing the system of inequality and injustice, in which the soul's life of self-realization and social status are limited to a significantly large part of the population. Social inequality infuses stratification, preconditioning the debacle of development.

CHAPTER 2:
Development Paths: Trajectories of Sociopolitical & Economic Reforms

DEVELOPMENT IS...

In today's world, where most governments are more concerned about economic growth rather than social equality and development, key questions arise on whether the decision-making apparatus leads to the improvement of people's lives. According to Rodrick (2010), very few nations put much emphasis on the social well-being of the masses. The decision-making process has raised contradicting thoughts on governments' commitment to raise society's social standards. In fact, as economic development is also measured on the basis of improving social indicators, governments find themselves in a quandary when assessing the outcome of investments. Ensuring that national projects benefit the population at large requires a careful consideration of society's needs prior to legislating any developmental decision.

SOCIAL DEVELOPMENT: ADVENT OF ECONOMIC GROWTH

Choy (1982) points out that studies on economic development reveal that the relationship between social gains and growth takes at least four different dimensions as follows:

1. Social development is a product of economic growth.
2. Social development always precedes economic growth.
3. Economic development and social development are unrelated events.
4. Neither social development nor economic growth is a primary cause of the other; instead, both are interdependent.

The first assessment on the relationship between social development and economic growth is central: many governments have widely adopted development policies that aim at improving the social well-being of citizens. However, as Naguib and Smucker (2009) point out, measuring economic growth is not only dependent on the society's welfare. It mostly focuses on related increases in consumption, investments, and savings. Consequently, not all emerging nations exhibit all the characteristics of economic development to prove that they are experiencing growth. GDP and GNP are two of the commonly employed indicators of economic advancement. Despite the fact that they can have a positive or negative impact on the social well-being of society, they have to be reflected in a nation's growth assessment for the country to be ranked as economically developed. Economic analysis cannot solely conclude that the results of growth evaluation mirror the situation on the ground when the measures of GNP or GDP per capita increase.

Secondly, GDP per capita does not show income distribution, especially among society's poor communities. Ailincă and Iordache (2013) describe that a country cannot qualify to be ranked as economically developed unless it achieves growth within the social status of its citizens. Accordingly, economic development is the only path through which nations can realize social equity and gains as economic and social developments are interrelated. Measures for achieving economic growth should consider the management of all factors that are related to social inclusion and citizens' development. Additionally, economic policies that effectively identify the means to enhance people's standards of living become integral for society's goals and contributory towards social gains. According to Moudatsou and Kyrkilis (2011), social goals including improvement of public resources and infrastructure cannot be achieved in a community or nation that is yet to actualize economic-growth objectives. Hereafter, social development in today's modern society comes as an advent of economic advancement.

As the third dimension claims, social development and economic growth are unrelated, mostly applicable to developing economies. That is, a handful of rich members in society utilize and consume public resources to continue amassing wealth, while the majority of the population at grassroots level wallow in poverty. Because of the existing disparity, nations are usually advised to put in place measures, which ensure that the economic development is felt even by the poorest members of society. In essence, this approach is only to achieve economic development that reflects improvement towards society's well-being as a whole.

The fourth dimension, however, argues that social development and economic growth are interdependent – a partially true assessment. The status of infrastructure, education and health institutions changes as a country continues to experience GDP growth. Similarly, an empowered society is usually motivated to work hard in order to achieve most of the economic development goals, set by its government (Moudatsou & Kyrkilis, 2011). Consequently, the two interdependent trajectories are derived from the outcomes of each other.

LIMITATIONS OF CONVENTIONAL GROWTH MODELS

Many countries today strive to achieve economic growth by applying conventional development models, but they fail to focus on key factors that dictate what economic advancement entails.

Investing in society itself translates into growth, which is the reason why economic strategists claim that development and social well-being are interrelated (Blanchet, 1991). However, most countries that do not possess the right formula or approach to achieve their objectives, as they tend to imitate and mimic the growth models that worked perfectly in other regions, fail to recognize the lack of capital and resources in order to realize the set goals. According to Fedderke and Klitgaard (1998), conventional development models require extensive land use for agricultural activities or extraction of minerals.

Because of its shortcomings, application of growth models is associated with high production costs of goods and services in many economies. These models are labor-intensive, and demand huge capital investments and technological resources, which are often out of reach for most developing countries. In fact, Clough (1955) points out that the real estate industry in many parts of the world exemplifies a sector, hugely influenced by those conventional growth models because investors utilize imported construction materials, raising the final mortgage values.

Conventional growth models often disregard non-economic specific elements including, namely, achieving a socially-empowered society or green – sustainable – growth. Lanzi and Delbono (2005) underline that the rate of economic development can be 'unsustainable' if countries do not consider the impact of the growth models that they apply. That is, many production activities today cause healthcare complications, leading to water scarcity, pollution, climate change, and loss of biodiversity. All these effects are irreversible, lowering nature's capability to sustain the needs of future generations. While global economy boasts innovation, which has essentially transformed traditional development methods, non-technological models can also be applied to help achieve sustainable development and sustainability as a growth trajectory (Lanzi & Delbono, 2005).

Although governments are required to transform land-use patterns by devising and applying ideal development plans, ensuring that the social gains meet the needs of all stakeholders in society becomes the ideal strategy. The use of capital and labor in industries should mirror and suit society's expectations. While capital-intensive business organizations are said to be more productive, only economies that have adequate resources benefit from the profits of these organizations. Fedderke (1997) advises that developing countries should assess their needs before setting targets for economic growth as well as the use of capital and labor. For instance, adopting models that increase savings helps in sustaining development and 'green' growth. It also supports countries to make positive changes to their economic structures, leading to the improvement of society's social welfare. Countries should overcome those challenges associated with achieving long-term economic goals through adopting better-suited, in-country specific development models instead of applying conventional techniques, which are deemed only effective in specific regions.

HUMAN DEVELOPMENT INDEX: A TOOL TO MEASURE SOCIETY'S ADVANCEMENT

By definition, human development index (HDI) is a tool used to measure the national development of a country, factoring in the level of knowledge, longevity and standard of living. These three factors are the basic elements of human development in which life expectancy measures the longevity. For instance, a combination of enrollment in learning institutions as well as adult literacy measures knowledge, while GDP per capita measures the standard of living. However, HDI is an economic tool employed to determine the non-income quality of life factors (Kamdar, & Basak, 2005). While HDI is a measure of national human development, it indicates whether a country is developing or not developing in the three following areas.

The necessity to create the HDI to measure human development started in the 1970s: partly as a response to the popularity of the dependency theory. This theory attributed poverty in some countries to exploitation by the wealthy (Kegley, & Blanton, 2013). Those advocating for the basic needs sought to have a new method of measuring the level of development among countries. As a result, HDI is slightly different from other tools that use economic indicators to determine the level of development (Ivanova, Arcelus, & Srinivasan, 1999). As a different tool of measuring development among countries, HDI determines the comparative ability of countries to provide for the well-being of their society's members in three key areas (Lind, 2004). A country ranking at the top of the HDI's table, for instance, is in a position to provide for the well-being of its citizens. On the contrary, a country ranking at the bottom of the HDI's table is not in a position to provide for society's well-being. Hence, countries appearing at the top of HDI table usually have a high life expectancy, high levels of education and high standards of living, yet those at the bottom have low levels of education, low standards of living and a low life expectancy.

The rationale of including educational attainment in the determination of HDI is that acquisition of knowledge helps in communicating and taking part in society's life. While acknowledging this fact, Lind (2019) claims that there may lack a statistical factor to measure the aptitude to participate in society's civic life. Despite the fact that only three factors appear to define HDI, many other elements may contribute to the definition. This simply means that these three factors, defining HDI, have other contributory elements that define them. In fact, Kamdar and Basak (2005) argue that HDI as a composite index refers to the different factors that define that index itself. That is, the effect of HDI is widespread, and it may impact many issues that determine human development. Lind (2019) explains that these HDI-defining factors may range between eight and twelve as a composite of indices, very sensitive to small changes of HDI components. Additionally, a change in one component may affect the HDI's ranking of other countries. As a result, HDI may invalidate the rankings, and it is important to justify parameters used by HDI in a rational manner.

ACHIEVING GROWTH, STABILITY & CONTINUITY: CONDITIONS & TERMS

In the quest for a few economies to realize and achieve sustainable development, preconditions are essential to guarantee growth, stability, and continuity. Most countries have come up with suitable strategies, which aim at evaluating their ability to maintain the pace of development that they are already experiencing (Sekhar, 2005). One of the preconditions of achieving long-term development is devising 'sustainable' visions by the country's leadership. According to Sekhar (2005), when the government is able to set achievable goals, it is likely that the country will lay down suitable policies to ensure that the vision becomes a reality. When China laid down its 25-year plan under the leadership of Deng Xiaoping, most people did not believe that remarkable transformations would be realized in the economy (Choy, 1982). Today, China's approach is arguably a suitable model for other developing nations that seek to achieve economic growth.

Another essential prerequisite to achieve a continued development cycle is political stability. Often, investors give a number of reasons to explain why they cannot seek opportunities with their hard-earned cash in countries of poor political systems. They go to places where they are guaranteed high returns, as well as a safe environment for employees to live – translating into capital flight and foreign direct investment. Unemployment, insecurity, and poverty become the order of the day in most countries with reduced investments, and economic development requires installing key transformative policies. Mazumdar (1996) points out that while most countries have plans for making the environment safe, research findings show that they fail to align their strategies with measures that promote political stability. Government institutions should demonstrate the willingness to implement policies that aim at enhancing transparency and participatory structures. If governmental agencies are incompetent and corrupt, it is unlikely that they will be held accountable for the in-country instability, discouraging investment continuity.

The final prerequisite is through enacting development policies that foster an overarching, cross-functional growth. Blanchet (1991) argues that socioeconomic structures are crucial pillars that determine whether a nation can sustain the rate of advancement that the country exhibits at any given time. As Chandra (2009) concurs and explains, society must provide its buy-in, endorsing the government's plans and projects – benefiting the community at large and contributing to the social welfare. Very often, national projects, devised abroad or drafted in-country, flop when society's needs, social expectations and cultural nuances are failed to be taken into account. Development strategies, focused on viable growth, environmental preservation and energy efficiency, for instance, have to align, employ and contribute to society's growth narratives and social goals – economic objectives alone are ill-prepared to benefit the whole.

POLITICAL INSTITUTIONS & INTEREST GROUPS: POLICY FORMULATION

Effective governance determines how authority in a country is exercised, and also plays an influential role in economic development and social stability. Mazumdar (1996) and Kanti (2008) argue that 'good' governance is an indispensable condition for developing a viable economic environment, which not only stimulates growth, but also ensures that society's living standards are improved. Additionally, interest groups, in charge of overseeing the government's activities, also play a critical role in guaranteeing the public that formulated policies are for the benefit of all members of society. These interest groups act as a mechanism to ensure that in-country policies lead to economic growth, while improving the standards of living and contributing to the social goals.

The Role of Political Institutions

According to Chua, Wong, & Shek (2010), policy-making and economic development are inseparable. Despite the involvement of many interest groups in rule-formulation processes, the government's framework is always influential in designing the economic system. Features of favorable policies for economic development include flexibility, coherence, stability, and the building of social capacities (Zagler, 2009; Kanti, 2008). These elements are essential because they enable leaders to put into effect rules that enhance economic development and political stability. Thus, every society should have an organized political system whose role is to maintain an ideal system for allocation and sharing of the country's resources.

Political institutions are deployed to formulate in-country laws, which guide society to take part in national development. Even in societies that do not have formal political structures, there is always a distinct decision-making authority, which dictates how rules are made and enacted. As many geopolitical regions grow wealthier, complex systems and political frameworks are developed to ensure that the interests of the majority in society are protected. In fact, Chua et al (2010) interestingly point out that the additional roles of the government include:

- Adopting and changing the elements of social, religious, and economic systems to achieve collective political goals.

- Enhancing the integration of society by determining its norms.
- Protecting the political system's integrity from external threats.

In essence, these three main roles are grouped into two categories. The first category describes the input function as management of political socialization, communication, and articulation of society's interests. Secondly, the output function entails rulemaking, application, and adjudication. Dependent on the governance-system type that is in place, Zagler (2009) underlines that, political institutions should ensure that the formulated policies create a conducive environment for business growth and economic development. Wealth-creation policies are required to transcend to the grassroots level of society, safeguarding that social development is beneficial to all classes of people.

The Role of Interest Groups

Key stakeholders in society including non-governmental organizations (NGOs), investors, businesses, multinational corporations (MNCs), and civil-society associations also have a role to play in the process of policy formation. These groups act as the governments' watchdog to ensure that the enacted policies help to improve society's well-being while delivering an equitable economic growth. As Fedderke, de Kadt, & Luiz (1999) explain, interest groups can also influence legislators to change, amend and nullify a policy if proven to be detrimental to the growth of the economy or society's welfare. In fact, international NGOs and MNCs, known for their vast investment in research and development (R&D), have a better understanding of how host-country governments can implement changes that stimulate economic growth. For instance, Pradhan, Mukhopadhyay, Gunashekar, Samadhan, & Pandey (2013) point out that international and in-country NGOs in developing economies can help the political leadership to identify gaps in the distribution of wealth and of resources, service delivery and strategy follow-up. Foreign investors and MNCs also have an impact on how host-country governments implement development policies. A country that seeks to benefit from foreign direct investment, MNCs' expertise and resource knowledge ensures that it sets favorable economic conditions including tax rebates, free-trade zones, joint-ventures, etc. In addition, the in-country policy should guarantee entrepreneurs that the business environment is favorable through the reduction of bureaucracy, inefficiencies, and corruption.

A country's infrastructure and security system are other crucial factors that foreign investors consider before making business decisions. Governments that fail to implement development policies lag behind in terms of road construction and energy generation. Clough (1955) explains that the in-country political leadership should not view foreign investments as a transactional procedure, but rather a venue for job creation and economic welfare. Additionally, civil-society associations are often a key partner in policy formation and also in incentivizing social capital, which creates collective action.

RETHINKING ECONOMIC GROWTH: SUSTAINABLE DEVELOPMENT

Developing or underdeveloped economies that seek to achieve long-term economic stability have to reconsider their growth strategies (Eisner, 1992). The implementation of suitable policies and reforms is essential for achieving economic and social advancement. According to Rodrick (2007), the United Nations Environmental Program (UNEP) has drafted key proposals to boost the global economy; to encourage employment; to reduce poverty and to accelerate the fight against environmental degradation and climate change, through essentially adopting green growth strategies. In its report, *Rethinking the Economic Recovery: A Global New Deal*, the UNEP recommends that countries should use a significant

portion of the available resources to invest in critical areas that guarantee maximum returns and achievement of a stable socioeconomic status (Pradhan et al., 2013). The five key strategy pillars in the proposal include:
- Energy efficiency.
- Adoption of renewable energy technologies.
- Overhaul of the transport industry by championing for the use of energy efficient means such as high-speed rails, hybrid cars, and rapid transit systems.
- Enactment of suitable agricultural reforms such as organic production and proper land use.
- Implementation of policies to improve the planet's ecology and preserve the status of freshwaters, forests, and soils.

While green growth strategies build on sustainability measures, ensuring the availability of resources for future generations, domestic and international policy architects are required to contribute to the long-term policy transition of creating stable global economy. As Rodrick (1993) underlines, these policies should aim at maintaining green growth while increasing the rate of economic development. However, additional reforms are needed in order to realize sustainability-driven growth, which include:

Improving Public Administration Sector

In-country administrative units play a pivotal role in determining the development path taken by a government. The political leadership are required to ensure that the in-country agencies are conversant with society's needs, social expectations and goals. Those agencies also need to be in a position to draft and develop directives that complement the government's efforts to transform society.

Changing the Role of the State

In the past, most in-country policies and growth strategies were developed by a central public administration body, and although this policy-making unit played an essential role in ensuring resource distribution, most grassroots initiatives were unachievable due to the lack of committed supervisory agencies. Therefore, while the central government focuses on policy formation, it is the responsibility of provincial administrations to oversee the implementation of the passed economic development measures. The change ensures that effective policies lead to the growth of all sectors that society as a whole considers essential.

Private Sector's Role: Social Gains

The private sector plays an active role in addressing socioeconomic issues affecting society at large. Eckersley (2009) argues that the private sector raises the 'happiness' factor of society, projecting income growth, and an increase in satisfaction or fulfillment of life – similarly to the expressed relative degree of indulgence – restraint. In fact, Eckersley (2009) further argues that Western developed economies with a dynamic private sector perform best within a 'subjective' well-being. That is, there exists a trend among society's members in developed economies to acquire knowledge and access resources that may help them improve their standards of living. This trend is widespread even though there are key socio-cultural values that society's members cherish, namely economic sociopolitical freedom.

Employing Technology

The advent of technological advancement, in its myriad forms including computerized information systems and data analysis, has streamlined the efficiency and accuracy of provisioning goods, services and resources. According to McBain and Alsamawi (2014), the appropriate use of technology leads to better productivity and greater transparency and objectivity.

Investing in Innovation

Today, innovation is a critical feature that improves economic performance, especially in developing economies. Chandra (2009) points out that continued research, development and innovation help address critical environmental, social and economic challenges. Through technological breakthroughs, many countries have managed to come up with new energy solutions that seek to reduce reliance on fossil fuels. Consequently, MNCs and host countries are able to reduce the costs of operations, and to redistribute resources.

In fact, innovation enables countries to develop better production methods, which ensure that industries demonstrate cost efficiency, resource effectiveness and improved service delivery. The increase in production capacity makes the latter possible for a country to earn foreign exchange capital by selling surplus commodities. Income, generated through these measures, can then be used to improve the healthcare sector and infrastructure, among others. Although the benefits of innovation are far-reaching, the process does not take place in a vacuum (Ailincă & Iordache, 2013). It requires the government to nurture a culture of creativity by increasing funding for implementing unique strategies, protecting intellectual property, and financing research and development projects that at the grassroots level are made to improve the existing system.

RETHINKING ECONOMIC GROWTH: CULTURAL DETERMINANTS

As economic development is determined by the decision-making process critical for growth – through market liberalization, increase of capital and investment, and development policy alignment, the existing socio-cultural reality of society presents a source of incubation for any decisions reached, while its societal setting fosters the necessary economic input for growth. However, stagnant growth in a number of markets can be explained by the failure of decision incubation and also the failure of recognizing social class differences, ill-suited for economic growth. Hofstede's six cultural dimensions benefits the analysis of society's socio-cultural impact on development and growth: these cultural dimensions underline and contextualize the societal setting, and Bowles (2008) argues that society's cultural setting should be flexible to accept and adapt to the effects of change. That is, uncertainty avoidance can be regarded as the essential cultural dimension, affecting and exercising force on the course of development and economic growth – a high or low cultural context will determine whether that society is ready to accept or resist change amidst the variation of its social classes.

Every culture is particular to its own societal setting, regionally or across borders, and culturally forms the basis of social, political, and economic policies. Any social change integrated along with its cultural reality is able to achieve society's ultimate goal (Smallbone & Welter, 2001). That is, prospective changes in society have to be consistent to the upheld values and norms. In effect, in order for in-country institutional policies to succeed and for the middle class to thrive, applying socio-culturally suitable objectives and measures are key to the integration process and are also instrumental in advancing development economically and socially. Barro and McCleary (2003) claim that self-determination is a value identification for development. Additionally, the system of governance is very much constitutive to the system of socioeconomic structure, matched against the rate of social mobility (Coyne & Williamson, 2009). However, as the process of globalization intensifies, reduced levels of upward social mobility hinder economic interactions (Platteau, 2000), and Coyne and Williamson (2009) reiterate that "in societies with lower levels of social capital, and hence lower levels of respect, the extent of the market will be limited to close kin and friendship networks" (p. 13). In essence, the intersection of individualism/collectivism, uncertainty avoidance and power distance appropriate economic development.

Notwithstanding, Barr and Glynn (2004) claim that the present variety of sociocultural norms and values existing in society across regions and national borders are a major source deterring economic development – also deterring the nuanced trajectory of sustainable development akin to socioeconomic viability. Accordingly, a society that has a hierarchical structure of governance often underpins conflict, lack of innovation and disparity. Interestingly, McSweeney (2002) points out that the United Kingdom has recorded a stunted growth during the 20th century because the culture of its upper social class resisted technological innovations and acquisition of knowledge. Barro and McCleary (2003) underline that Latin American cultures are a prime example of a societal context, mainly characterized as promoting a "culture of poverty," a Western misconception and misbelief. However, international institutions, including the World Bank and the Organization for Economic Co-operation and Development (OECD), play a critical role as a source of influencing the discourse of development and its trajectory path, through introducing, lobbying and/or generating a new system of values and governance, assumed eventually by growth. Therefore, the socio-cultural reality of society has a correlative relation to the discourse of development, despite other fiscal and monetary factors.

THE NEW FRONTIER IS...

There does not exist a single universal plan to achieve development. Although innovation, policy alignment and socio-culturally-driven sustainability measures may provide the necessary tools to devise the development strategy a country needs, the societal dynamics within its social context of classes creates the trajectory of development. Social mobility becomes the central frontier of development – regardless of its political, social or economic trajectories. The narrative of development has to be revised and changed to address the in-country socially-specific cultural realities: development becomes a leverage for economic advancement, while social mobility enhances the development of a healthy middle class. The middle class would then maintain the continuity of development trajectories.

CHAPTER 3
Middle Class Engineering: Upward Social Mobility

SOCIAL STRUCTURE

The social structure of modern society is a consequence of event-specific socioeconomic changes. The past decades depict the conception of a socioeconomic phenomenon, lionized within a social structure: i.e., the rise of the middle class. Although the contentions of class division and stratification have greatly contributed to the socioeconomic theory and sociopolitical discourse, the middle class – the rise, decline or the lack thereof, has become the central, salient indicator of growth-specific trajectory within a country's development path.

As class division intensifies in a given society, the presence of certain grades of social ranking becomes a contributory positive factor for the in-country course of development – progress then becomes indicative and determinant of socioeconomic stature and society's well-being.

For a long time, historians and sociopolitical thinkers continue to contest and dispute the causes of class division, and the composition of classes in a particular social stratum. The current body of knowledge builds on existing changes flowing through the analysis of individual classes (high, middle, low) with their inherent characteristics. A research of class division in society is the basis for the study of a particular social grouping, and its relevance encircles the middle class as a social structure.

MIDDLE CLASS: FUNCTIONALITY

The theoretical framework associated and applied with middle class analysis examines its functionality as a social grouping and its uncertainty as a class position in modern society. In its analytical context, the middle class can be identified by, and can assume the following features: property criterion, a certain level of education, the criterion of the intellectual nature of work, as well as the criterion of self-identification. The middle class — a rather specific, heterogeneous socioeconomic concept – is considered as the 'core and as the periphery units' in society (Lu, 2005). Lu (2005) describes the 'core units' as a class 'basic' of the specified number of citizens or a group, and those core units cover all those people who have all the criteria of the middle class. 'Peripherals' can be divided into neighboring – as the presence of all the criteria with the lowest values – and remote/distance – corresponding to the present of at least one criterion. In its qualitative features, the middle class symbolizes the most economically active pressure groups, created of entrepreneurs, public servants, technocrats, scientists, employees of private enterprises, senior heads of organizations…etc.

In fact, the middle class is non-uniform due to the substantial differences within the group, and Zeitlin (1974) defines the 'decision makers,' as public servants, technocrats and all of those within the political machinery of the state; antagonists are scientists, intellectual and creative elites, and civil-society associations; key stakeholders and the main protagonists are employees of private enterprises, senior heads of organizations, large transnational/multinational corporations…etc. In essence, the middle class remains flexible, and is able to respond and to adapt to any changes, and also to develop further, providing technological and socioeconomic progress. Wheary (2010) argues that the middle class has a special human-capital development, without which the existence of a class is impossible.

As a social grouping within socioeconomic structures, the middle class possesses a complex and heterogeneous character, evident in developed economies from the time when social division of society became necessary, and the creation of a new socioeconomic structure appeared. The middle class primarily performs social and economic functions, endorsing or criticizing in-country policies. The middle class in itself acts as a socioeconomic guarantor of the progressive development in society, and also increases upward social mobility trend, encouraging the transition from one social layer to another.

As characterized by complexity yet heterogeneity, the middle-class phenomenon became widespread during the industrial and post-industrial stages of social development. However, the middle class can also be defined as a unified socially-integral grouping, whose socioeconomic structures share common characteristics in a system of dominance: i.e., education, income....etc. The formation of middle class contributes to the development of economic spectrums, as well as to particular political activities of the in-country governance direction. In fact, society's class division is the result of social construction; namely due to how the analysis and interpretation of economic and social conditions influence human existence and society. Hence, these analytical constructions may vary, creating methodological differences. Giddens (1984, 1991) argues in his theory of structuration that middle-class semantic content differs depending on changes within the socioeconomic life of any country. Giddens (1984) points out that most sociologists focus on explaining the youth of the middle-class stratum, as "tacitly enacted practices" which "reproduce familiar forms of social life" (p. 94). The latter forms a new middle class as Giddens (1991) further explains.

NEW MIDDLE CLASS

The distinguished American sociologist Charles Wright Mills once argued that the main difference between the 'old middle class' and the 'new one' is reflected in the fact that the latter was made of small entrepreneurs, most of whom have owned the right to gain profits and to generate an income. Unlike Europe, the American middle class was dedicated to the bucolic bourgeoisie, owning the land and controlling the means of production, and the means of earnings and investment. As described by Mills (1951), in order for a small entrepreneur to use his land for investment, determining the investment criteria and terms is a prerequisite to receive professional duties and rights. Thus, the entrepreneurial exercise is carried out solely and independently by the entrepreneur forming a new middle class. In opposite, the 'old middle class,' as Mills (1951) points out, was first identified with accordance to the criteria of ownership and private property. Secondly, its frames, although remained penetrable, were legibly defined, and thirdly, they didn't depend on neither the state policy, nor on the upper class by virtue of a personified, entrepreneurial employment (Horowitz, 1964).

Additionally, as Kingston (2000) argues, despite all the analytical and political struggles among researchers of classes, they share the basic views of social structure. The primary principle is that stratification within the social system consists of a limited and eligible number of separate groups – "classes that are determined and managed by their independent economic position" (p. 5). In fact, Mills (1951) underlines that the control over economic and finance resources are of central importance for Marxists and Weberians. Mills (1951) argues that both Marx and Weber would agree that the middle class can and should be defined by its economic positioning, and the followers of the Marxist and Weberian methodology diverge stylistically. Their criteria, due to the sociological tradition, need to be revised as they are outdated.

Alternative terminologies to 'middle class' are repelled from total statements: the notion of class as a separate social grouping, defined by economic criteria, is outdated; the blurred boundaries between classes and class ideology can no longer be considered an adequate tool of analysis of social relations. Critics of class ideology do not deny the existence of class boundaries, including the conventional boundaries between people of different economic structures in society, but argue that classes, first, do not always coincide with the boundaries of inequality, and, secondly, that class identity is an indicator of a person's position in the hierarchy of income and, possibly, in the labor market, but has a limited impact on his/her consciousness, life experience or political position. Proponents of class identity argue not so much about the principle of the separation of people into groups based on economical production characteristics, but on the conviction that these dividing lines are directly reflected in other social, cultural or political-ideological spheres of life.

Anti-class ideology, pioneered by Robert Nisbet in the 1959 *'The Decline and Fall of the Concept of Social Class'* is experiencing a recent revival. In the 1995 *'Death of Class,'* formulated by Jan Pakulski and Malcolm Waters, classes are blurred, and the most developed societies are no longer class-divided, with the consequence that the type of analysis, in which class seemed to explain some category, must give way to the more open, not having a predefined objective of social analysis (Pakulski & Waters, 1995). Jan Pakulski and Malcolm Waters argued that class is an outdated concept, unable to express the novelty of the current social forms and relations.

Additionally, Kingston (2000) points out that the 'class' nature of American society is not confirmed by empirical data. He argues that class analysis in American sociology serves as a language to describe the phenomenon of inequality, but classes, themselves, as objective phenomena of social life, in determining the interests and lifestyle of society, do not exist. Instead of class ideology or terminology, Kingston (2000) proposes to examine the social order as an overlapping economic hierarchy of ranks and as fragmented, changing clots of cultural strata. Kingston's convictions validate the fact that the commonality of people's economic conditions along with the similarity of their life experiences, based on class identity, has been blurred under the influence of new circumstances to which it relates economic diversification, contributing to the heterogeneity of classes, to a high level of social mobility, solvent class boundaries, coupled with technological advancements. The increase in the diversity of employment types, labor-market figures, multiple levels of responsibility and accountability does not allow to clearly define the criteria of middle class, forcing academic research to discuss social grades (Kingston, 2000).

MIDDLE CLASS ENDANGERED

Throughout the course of history in developed economies, the middle class has acted as the guarantor of social and political stability, combining strong economic positioning with political moderation, if not passive. Today, the middle class in these economies, especially in the United States, is in danger. Scholars and researchers are sounding the alarm, attracting the attention of the public to the fact that the middle class is dying, and Pressman (2007) suggests that the problem of middle-class decline and disappearance merits a separate line of research. Policy makers have recognized that the middle class is on the verge of extinction (Pressman, 2007).

Fry and Kochhar (2014) examine the wealth gap between US middle- and upper-income households – as illustrated in Figure 3.1.

Figure 3.1:

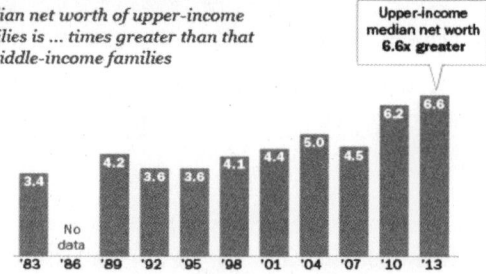

Source: Fry, R. & Kochhar, R. (2014). *America's wealth gap between middle-income and upper-income families is widest on record*. Retrieved on 07 May 2015 from: http://www.pewresearch.org/fact-tank/2014/12/17/wealth-gap- upper-middle-income/

As depicted in Figure 3.1, the economic conditions, ceasing the existence of the middle class are quickly deteriorating, leading to erosion and reduction in the population size, while upper profit-net worth was 6.6 times bigger in 2013, in comparison to middle profit-net worth. The social and economic polarization breaks middle-class solidity, on the lines of social tension between oppositely charged poles of wealth and poverty (Fry & Kochhar, 2014).

Table 3.1:

Only Upper-Income Families Have Made Wealth Gains in Recent Decades

Median household net worth by income, 2013 dollars

	ALL FAMILIES	LOWER INCOME	MIDDLE INCOME	UPPER INCOME
2013	$81,400	$9,300	$96,500	$639,400
2010	82,300	10,500	96,500	595,300
2007	135,700	18,000	158,400	718,000
2001	114,100	19,100	134,200	590,300
1992	80,800	13,800	94,100	338,500
1983	76,600	11,400	94,300	318,100

Source: Fry, R. & Kochhar, R. (2014). *America's wealth gap between middle-income and upper-income families is widest on record*. Retrieved on 07 May 2015 from: http://www.pewresearch.org/fact-tank/2014/12/17/wealth-gap-upper-middle-income/

As detailed in Table 3.1, the 2013 middle class family's income is almost six times lower than upper class families. The gap is incredible, as the difference is increasingly growing. The gravitational area of these poles is so great that the middle class begins to be structured within itself, as if stretching itself along the axis of the wealth – poverty.

Figure 3.2:

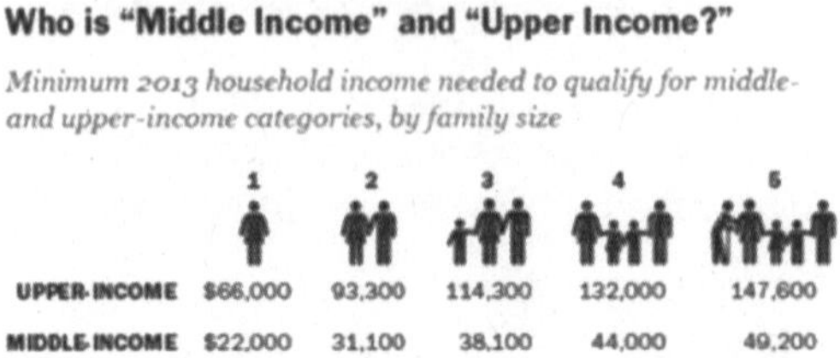

Who is "Middle Income" and "Upper Income?"

Minimum 2013 household income needed to qualify for middle- and upper-income categories, by family size

Family size	1	2	3	4	5
UPPER-INCOME	$66,000	93,300	114,300	132,000	147,600
MIDDLE-INCOME	$22,000	31,100	38,100	44,000	49,200

Source: Fry, R. & Kochhar, R. (2014). *America's wealth gap between middle-income and upper-income families is widest on record.* Retrieved on 07 May 2015 from: http://www.pewresearch.org/fact-tank/2014/12/17/wealth-gap-upper-middle-income/

Figure 3.2 shows that, in practice, the self-structure of middle class exhibits the fact that part of this social grouping overcomes economic challenges, by approaching the highest, while the latter part is impoverished – tightened by the working or a lower class. For instance, income for a family of different sizes is up to 2-3 times lower than of an upper-class family of the same size. Polarization property inside the middle-class group leads to the indication that its economic fundamentals are blurred.

In analyzing the U.S. middle-class share within the American national income, as shown in Figure 3.3, Miller and Madland (2014) point out that this share, in itself, had been rapidly decreasing from 53.2% in 1967 to 45.8% in 2013 (p. 1). In fact, Miller and Madland (2014) argue that the U.S. middle class is shrinking due to mobility, and is directionally upward and downward – indicatively unsteady. Accordingly, its reduction is not only due to the fall, but also due to the growth of the welfare of its members.

Figure 3.3:

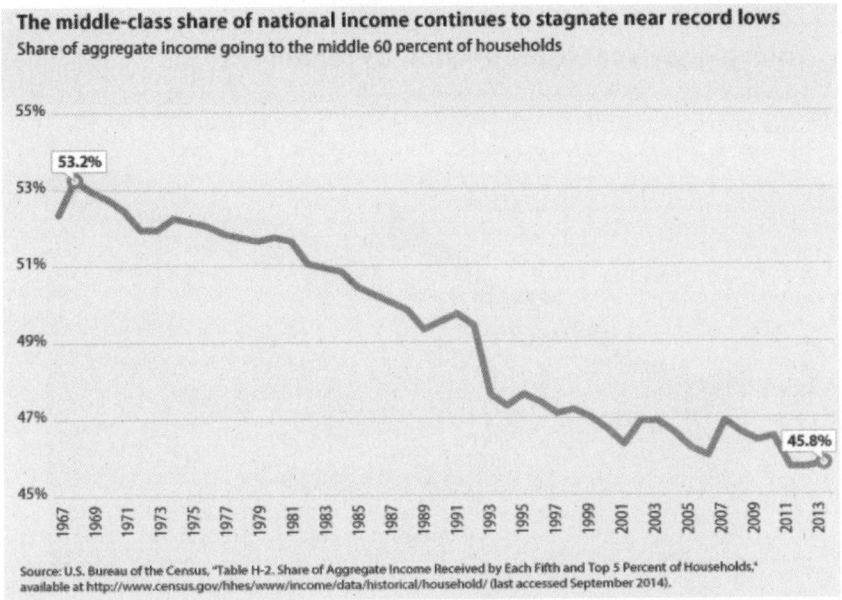

Source: Miller, K. & Madland, D. (2014). *What the New Census Data Show about the Continuing Struggles of the Middle Class*. Retrieved on 07 May 2015 from: https://www.americanprogress.org/issues/economy/news/2014/09/16/97203/what-the-new-census-data-show-about-the-continuing-struggles-of-the-middle-class/

Internationally, as depicted in Research Institute Credit Suisse's figures 3.4.A and 3.4.B, the prolonged global economic crisis, within the years of 2012-2014, led to a decline of incomes within the global middle class, yet particularly in the United States – with the level of income of U.S. middle class families ranking 27th. To account for the number of millionaires, billionaires and multi-billionaires, America would rank first in the world, and similarly on the total value of assets of the richest on a growing GDP. According to Research Institute Credit Suisse's (2014) study, "the global value of median wealth per adult [is set] to rise by 36%, from U.S. $3,600 today to U.S. $5,000 in 2019. While the number of adults with wealth below U.S. $10,000 will shrink by 1%, the number will rise by 30% in the middle-class wealth range, and by 20% in the upper class-middle band" (p. 42).

Figure 3.4.A:

Total global wealth 2000–2014, by region

Source: James Davies, Rodrigo Lluberas and Anthony Shorrocks, Credit Suisse Global Wealth Databook 2014

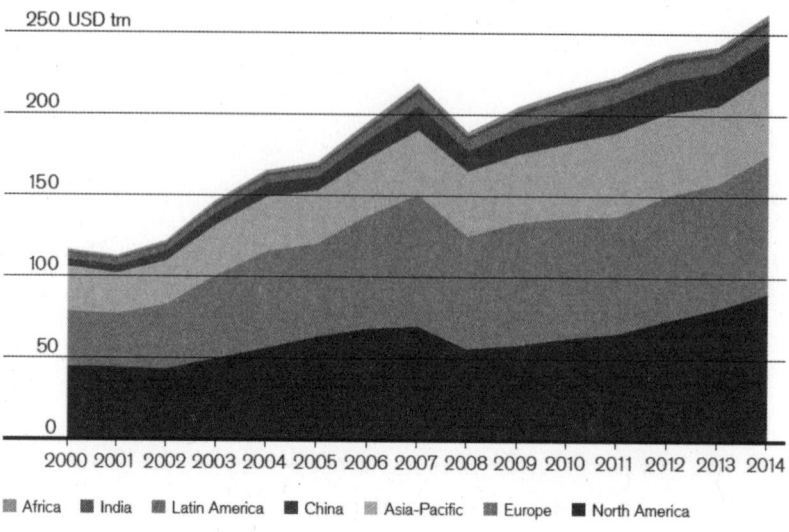

Figure 3.4.B:

Source: James Davies, Rodrigo Lluberas and Anthony Shorrocks, Credit Suisse Global Wealth Databook 2014

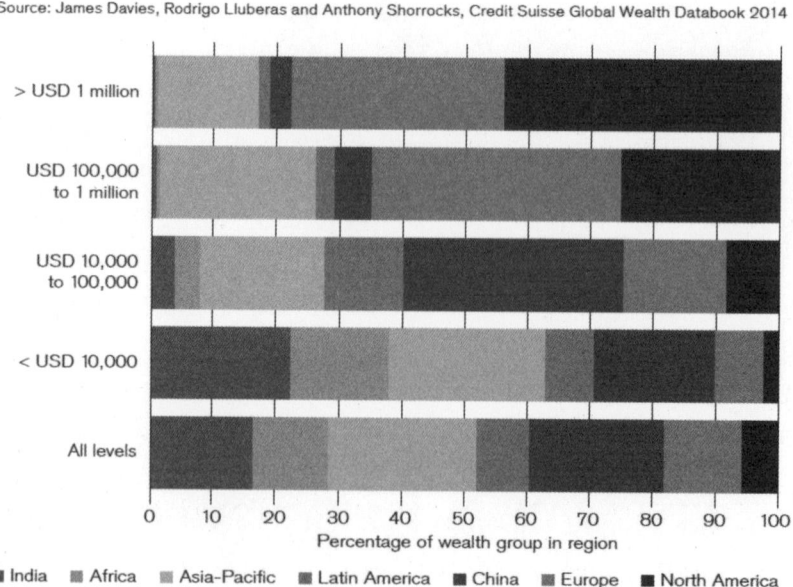

Figure 3.4.C:

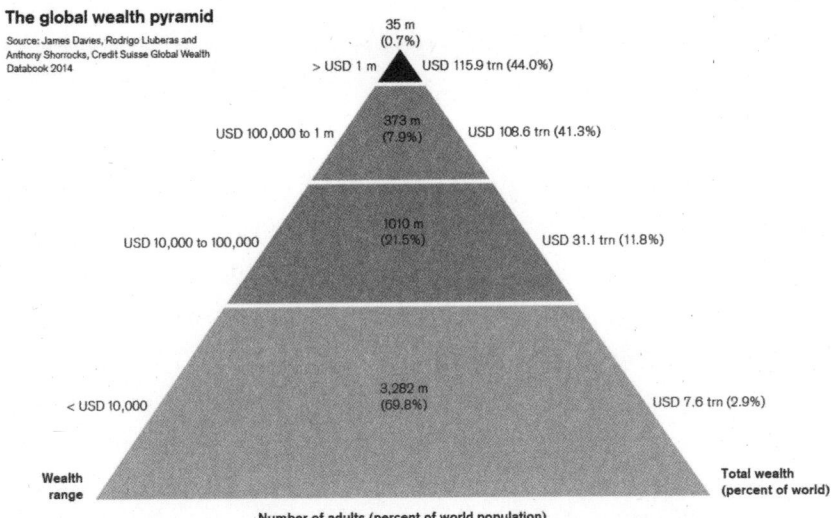

Source: Research Institute Thought leadership from Credit Suisse Research and the world's foremost experts. (2014). Global Wealth Databook 2014. Retrieved on 07 May 2015 from: http://economics.uwo.ca/people/davies_docs/credit-suisse-global-wealth-report-2014.pdf

MIDDLE CLASS: ECONOMIC SECURITY

Higher degrees of economic and political balance in modern market economies are orchestrated through and by a stable social formation – the middle class. In the system of economic security, the middle class possesses primary decisive power. Weller and Logan (2009) argue that this power is due to its functional features in targeting economic activities; contributory to a stable governing state/country. In fact, among the middle-class functional features in the system of economic security, priority is owned by stabilizing, consolidating, and harmonizing innovative functions, where the latter is inherent in redistribution of investment and business sector activities. Weller and Logan (2009), and Kaufman (2005) identify key directions for the middle class to influence economic security. These include:

1. Further innovation, increasing the share of expenditures on research and development.
2. Increased investments by the ratio of own sources of financing.
3. Better quality of life along with the increase in gross domestic and gross national/regional product per capita.
4. Developing small and medium enterprises contributes to the stability of the production process, and increases competitiveness, in order to meet the needs of the population.
5. Developing in-country programs addressing social inequality, income gaps, and taxation.
6. Social buffering, preventing societal tensions.

Hence, the in-country systems by which the middle class influences its economic security determine the country's socioeconomic stability. Thus, stability becomes a structural advantage of middle-class economic security.

MIDDLE CLASS: ITS UNIQUE UTILITY

The middle class plays a unique societal role, defined within economic independence/ entrepreneurship and professional/career orientation, which characterize a highly-valued, rewarding society. The latter becomes the mechanism in which the middle class can expand and thrive. Accordingly, Kaufman (2005) argues that although the basic, or rather, the primary function of the middle class is social utility, societal stability is a function of the existing social structure in which the middle class ceases to exist. Thus, the middle class is a system 'stabilizer,' and once social structures are achieved, the middle class devises its grouping and positioning by exercising specific socioeconomic leverage. Kaufman (2005) points out that in the process of upward social mobility, the middle class ascertains the existing social order, protected from societal cataclysms: the discontent of the lower class is balanced by real opportunities to improve 'status' within society. The larger the middle class is, the lower the probability becomes that society will bear revolutions, ethnic conflicts, and social upheavals. Subsequently, the middle class separates two opposite poles, poor and rich, and makes them collide. The lower the middle class is, the closer to each other the polar points of stratification are, making their collision more likely.

A key social utility of middle class in countries with market economy is its role in the process of vertical mobility. Major social movements in society occur within the middle class, and between other elements of the social structure. The middle class creates an unrestricted channel of upward vertical mobility, a clear perspective of social growth, the base of which is education, health and qualifications, ensuring a high level of welfare. Kaufman (2005) underlines that 'immigrants' from the middle class join the upper class while the social-grouping middle class welcomes those members of society, who have managed to overcome social and economic barriers. In fact, middle-class economic behavior is dependent on the type of market economy, with regular assessment of its qualities. Within this context, the middle class plays the role of an economic donor – not only as a producer of a huge part of disposable income in society, but also as a large consumer-based, investment-driven and tax-paying tier. The middle-class disposable income is the basis of solvency in the socioeconomic structure, and also creates opportunities to further develop the domestic economy, which may often be constrained by insufficient demand.

MIDDLE CLASS: TODAY'S REALITY

In the highly developed economies, the middle class is the primary carrier of public interest, and possesses a national culture characterized by society's values, norms, and beliefs. The middle class shares and spreads models of its own culture in the upper and lower layers of society. Hence, culturally, the grouping middle class acts as a social integrator of a specific society. The middle class consumes on a massive scale, not only a verity of goods and services, but also products of culture. The grouping is, thus, a major producer and consumer of 'mass urban culture.' In essence, the middle class is the main political base of power. Wheary (2010) points out that the middle class has a very strong, and sometimes decisive, influence on the adoption of particular economic and political decisions in the policy of the ruling elite, which does not listen to the majority's 'voice.'

However, in the aftermath of the global financial crisis, revealing the inefficiency of the international economic paradigm, it is difficult to predict how the middle class can survive and persevere, since this social grouping has always served as a guarantor of societal stability and sociopolitical harmony in developed economies. Today, the middle class in these societies, especially in the United States, is in danger. Today's middle class is deteriorating as a result of a variety of political, economic and social challenges, including, namely, the attempt to adapt to the escalating global competition and to overcome key financial and economic disparities.

SUSTAINABLE DEVELOPMENT: EMPOWERED BY A GROWING MIDDLE CLASS

A thriving middle class preconditions development, and strengthens the country's economy – a prerequisite for a robust economic outlook. Additionally, a conscientious middle class empowers the variant spectrum of social classes to seize entrepreneurial opportunities, and also directs policy drafting towards a sustainability-integrated economic outlook. In fact, sustainability enables the necessary stewardship of structural and institutional changes, production methods, and effective governance system, creating an ultra-mechanism through which the social classes can avert economic exploitation, and can foster a conducive value system of embracing economic growth, and socio-cultural integrity. If sustainable development is fully embraced, and empowered by the middle class, society's economic goals and socio-cultural objectives can hereafter be achieved in a moral, governance-specific, fiscally responsible upright fashion. That is, sustainability, if cherished by a politically strong middle class, brings together and seemingly aligns divergent policies and structures to converge into a core governance strategy, serving long-term socioeconomic goals.

In its socio-cultural reality, society's propensity to cope with change and with innovation forms the integral principle of development. Sustainability offers the necessary leverage of innovation to combat market shortcomings, and to maintain continuity. Devising and introducing culturally-specific measures, to encourage a productive economic outlook and a proactive relationship with the varying social classes, depend on the course of development that the in-country leadership, political institutions and interest groups recognize and jointly support. While the socio-cultural reality of society predisposes the path of development, the correlative attitude of social classes, namely the middle class, encourages sustainability discourse and the course of socioeconomic development.

CHAPTER 4:
Post-Socialist, New Capitalist Serbia: Middle Class Formation

POST SOCIALISM

To date, within the period of post-socialist countries, 'transition' reforms have always intended to complete the process of forming a new social structure in society. These reforms not only affect society's system of stability, but also attempt to customize country-specific socioeconomic strategies. In developed economies, the middle class represents this country-specific strategy interlocutor, and its share covers no less than two-thirds of the main social classes. However, post-socialist economies are formed by a social structure that maintains only a partly adequate share of middle class, incomparable to that of developed economies. The Republic of Serbia, as a post-socialist, new capitalist economy, has recently drawn the attention of cross-cultural, sociopolitical, market liberalism research studies. Although confronted with key methodological challenges including the lack of data, which could allow tracing the dynamics and correlations of certain variables during the transformational period, Serbia represents a peculiar in-country case of developing the middle class in a new capitalistic order, overlaid with culturally-specific socialistic values.

As social classes evolve and become complex, Berberoglu (2007) argues that the economic structures condition the social and political orders. The middle class then orchestrates the 'success' or 'stability' of these orders in the construction of a liberalized market economy post-1989. Berberoglu (2007), in fact, points out that this process clearly falls into three parts: post-socialistic, transformational and post-transformational. The period of 1990-2000 in Serbia was tightly connected to Milošević's era, described as blocked, or delayed modernization. Lazic and Cvejic (2011) underline that during the 1990-2000 period, Serbia along with other countries in the Balkan region created mass conversions of political power and social order. In Serbia, two-thirds of its business organizations in the first half of the 1990s were controlled by kinship and family ties, and had continued supporting the former authoritarian-collective culture. 'Unlocked' or open channels of upward mobility took place only after the completion process of post-socialist transformation, incubating the growth of Serbia's middle class.

The issues of social structures were first articulated by Karl Marx and his theory, defined as the problem of minimal social structures – the minimum number of social groups, and the interaction of which determines how these groups develop. Milios (2000) argues that the hierarchical structure, founded by Marxism, is hidden behind the vertical stratification of the source of social differences, lying on the horizontal plane: the division into classes, in general; and the bipolar structure of economic relations, in particular – the ownership of the means of production and the deprived labor force. In class structure dynamics, 'destruction of classes' remains the gradual displacement from public life, dividing society into hostile classes and determining the class character of the ruling elite, to complex social contradictions. O'Hara (2000) further argues that a society of 'ravaged' strata is a society that supersedes the class dichotomy and that lacks the resources to resolve conflicts between social grouping and integration.

SERBIA'S MIDDLE CLASS: RESTRICTIVE SOCIAL MOBILITY

In Serbia's middle class, the ensued period of socialism or authoritarian collectivism has predisposed this social group culture. Thus, the values of authoritarian collectivism have become normative in the culture of Serbia's middle class, and socially challenging to break down in the post-social era (Morley, 1983). In the 1990s, for those members of Serbia's lower-class social layer, the process of transition into the ranks of economic elitism – middle class, was sealed. Lazic and Cvejic (2011) point out that the 1989-1990 period witnessed no resistance to the then status-quo, while the period of 1991-1997 showcased an attempt by Serbia's elites to maximize the benefits of their existing socioeconomic stature; yet, the 'unlock' transformation post-1997, and especially in 2000, pushed for developing a market-led economy, ensuring property rights. However, Lazic and Cvejic (2011) further argue that top social-class layers were 'closed,' and belonged to the economic elite social grouping which became hereditary. Lazic and Cvejic (2011) explain that social mobility partially remained closed, and the transition from class to class was still difficult. The process of class reconstruction has concluded, but most of Serbia's middle-class members remain closely associated with and enchanted by the period and culture of socialism and authoritarian collectivism.

Lazic and Cvejic (2011) reiterate that Serbia's social class inter-relationship, and its networks continue to play a significant role in the country's, arguably, liberalized market economy. In fact, Daskalovic (2015) expects Serbia's economy to shrink, and explains, as detailed in Table 4.1, that Serbia's Gross Domestic Product (GDP) average rate declined in 2015 by -0.5%, and was -0.2 in 2014. The Economist Intelligence Unit (EIU) (2015) forecasts similar projections on Serbia's economy, and Serbia's GDP is projected to gradually increase reaching around 2.5-3% in 2016 and 3.2-3.7% in

2017, which will affect the conditions of Serbia's economy and its continued efforts to develop its middle class.

Table 4.1:

	2014	2015	2016	2017	2018	2019
GDP	-2	-0.5	2.8	3.7	3.8	3.6
Consumer prices	2.9	3.3	4.5	4.5	4.5	4.5
Current balance (% of GDP)	-4.5	-4.2	-4.2	-4	-4.1	-4.3
Government budget (% of GDP)	-4.7	-4.4	-4	-3.7	-3.5	-3.4
Short-term interest rates (%)	7.5	7	6.6	6.5	6.5	6.5
Exchange rate (LC per US$)	88.4	98.1	100.3	102.1	104	105.9

Source: Daskalovic, Dj. (2015). SeeNews. The Corporate Wire. Serbia's 2015 GDP seen down 0.5%, to rebound in 2016 – EY. Retrieved on 02 June 2015 at: http://wire.seenews.com/news/serbias-2015-gdp-seen-down-0-5-to-rebound-in-2016-ey-469550

Table 4.2:

Economic growth %	2014[a]	2015[b]	2016[b]	2017[b]	2018[b]	2019[b]
GDP	-1.8[c]	-0.2	2.5	3.2	3.7	4.0
Private consumption	-1.3	-0.6	1.4	2.0	3.0	3.0
Government consumption	-0.9	-0.8	1.0	1.6	1.7	2.0
Gross fixed investment	-3.4	-1.0	3.0	5.2	6.0	5.0
Exports of goods & services	4.0	6.6	5.0	6.3	6.5	7.0
Imports of goods & services	3.2	1.0	3.0	4.3	6.3	6.3
Domestic demand	-1.5	-2.2	1.7	2.4	3.8	3.9
Agriculture	1.5	3.0	2.0	2.3	2.0	2.0
Industry	-7.0	-2.0	2.0	4.0	5.0	5.0
Services	1.5	0.9	2.0	2.4	2.9	3.6

[a] Economist Intelligence Unit estimates. [b] Economist Intelligence Unit forecasts. [c] Actual.

Source: The Economist Intelligence Unit. (2015). Country Report: Serbia.

EIU (2015) expects that emerging markets will experience strong growth within the next 2-3 years, yet the forecast for a number of countries remains unclear. Ernest & Young (EY) (2014) claim that the Serbian government is taking steps to restore the pace of its economic development, and EY (2014) point to the fiscal trend of growth acceleration in fast-growing markets including Poland and the Czech Republic as an attempt to increase in-country industrial capacities. EY (2014) argue that the dynamic growth of the middle class – the economic class that increasingly consume different goods and services, will become a determinant criterion in the rise of domestic demand of emerging markets. In the short, near term, Serbia is to benefit from a lot of advantages (EIU, 2015). The growth of its middle class will contribute to a significant increase in demand for services in health and education, which will lead to improved workforce skills within these sectors. The increase in the cost of communications services, culture, leisure and entertainment will outpace the growth of expenditure on food by more than half (EY, 2014).

Daskalovic (2015) predicts that in the next decade, the demand growth for consumer products subsidiary will outpace the growth in demand for basic goods. However, to leverage the benefits of middle-class growth against the balanced use of scarce resources in a growing and developing economy, investments in research and development, technological breakthroughs including sustainability measures and green technologies, and public infrastructures begin to improve the in-country business environment and regulatory framework. Daskalovic (2015) further argues that with relatively low growth in financial and business services, short-term interest rates are predicted to be at 7% in 2015 while the 2015 exchange rate will be 98.1%. Serbia's current balance is expected to drop to -4.2% this year.

Daskalovic's (2015), EIU's (2015) and EY's (2014) forecasts call for the development of industry-specific trends as urbanization has increased the demand for retail goods and other consumer services. With relative high degrees of uncertainty in the financial markets, Serbia's economy may face capital outflows and a weaker national currency. In several accounts, fiscal uncertainty or a low level of economic growth can lead to the reluctance of investors to take more risks and may result in the outflow of portfolio investment from emerging markets or countries in which the funding deficit of the current account depends on the inflow of portfolio investments – for instance, Serbia. EY (2014) argue that the capital outflow will lead to higher inflation, interest rates and debt burden, which will stifle economic growth. Additionally, reducing prices of shares and residential property will limit the potential to further grow developing markets (EY, 2014). In essence, the experience of developed countries depicts that the dynamics and opportunities of socially-oriented innovation development is largely determined by the position of the middle class, its size, structure and capacity to implement its economic interests and capital (Fedderke & Klitgaard, 1998).

SERBIA: CULTURAL PARADIGMS

Hofstede (1980) defines culture as a collective programing of the mind. It distinguishes one category of society's members from another. To exercise Hofstede's cultural dimensions, Serbia is taken as a case against a similar socio-politically-oriented culture of Vietnam – two countries with economies in transition, existing within different religious branches, cultures, but are related to relatively similar political and economic subsystems. One of the main theoretical frameworks being employed in analyses of a country's culture today is the Hofstede's cultural dimensions – as described and detailed in my introduction.

Figure 4.1:

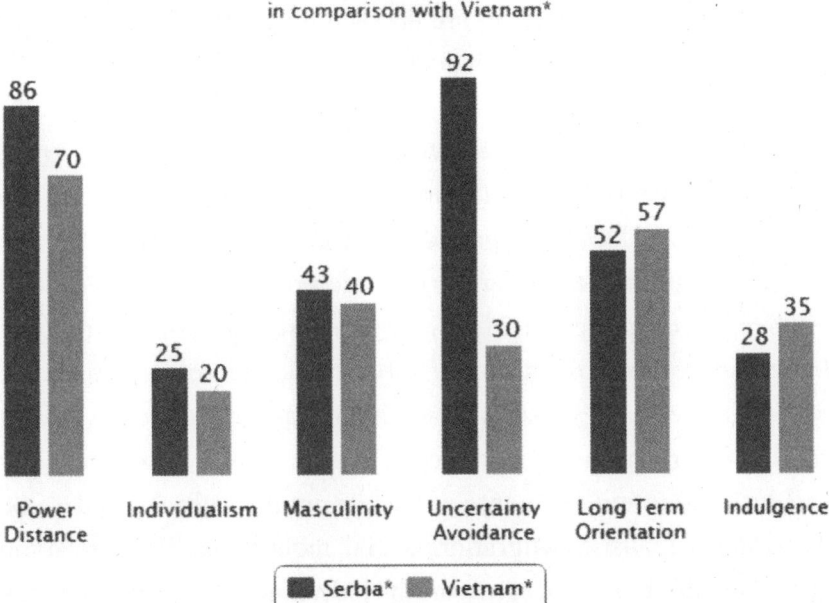

Source: Hofstede (1980)

In its historical context, Eastern Europe and the Balkan region had weak ties with the Occident – the West, as largely been associated with the Ottoman Empire, influenced by authoritarian collectivism yet practiced a more conservative in-group orientation of Orthodox Christianity. Vietnam lives within the vestiges of Confucian collectivism, influencing the values of its society today. Within the case of Serbia against Vietnam, these factors help explain the relatively weak Individualism (25), Indulgence (28), yet concurrently very high ranks for Uncertainty Avoidance (92), Long Term Orientation (52) and Power Distance (86). Vietnam, however, demonstrates the pragmatism and focuses slightly more on entrepreneurship – correlated by Masculinity at (40). Although this orientation is combined with a bright expression of Power Distance (70) and with the denial of Indulgence (35) and Individualism (20), to go in depth, Hofstede's country's cultural profile coincides with the research studying the cultures of Serbia and Vietnam while the regional, internal differences are deemed invariable. However, both countries have relatively high degrees of collectivism; (75) for Serbia and (80) for Vietnam.

Conversely, Uncertainty Avoidance, ranking (92) in Serbia, becomes the central cultural paradigm in cross-examining Serbia's in-country development against new capitalist countries. That is, future apprehensiveness and risk intolerance are infused in a relatively masculine, highly centralized sociopolitical structure. Interestingly, Pinillos and Reyes (2011) argue that society's financial well-being leads to social and psychological independence, giving rise to the formation and presence of middle class. The most affluent and most educated segments of society in any culture tend to be more individualistic. Migration, social mobility and urbanization also contribute to the growth of individualism. However, the manifestation of individualistic or collectivistic tendencies depends not only on culture, but also on the social context.

SOCIOECONOMIC MODERNIZATION: POST-SOCIALIST SERBIA

Throughout its history, Serbia has gone through a modernization transition from one development path to a new model of economic growth. Its modernization tasks are very different in their own modes of in-country institutional and economic structures. Serbia and Vietnam exemplify two countries that have undertaken modernization breakthroughs, and have suffered from shortcomings in the process of developing social classes. In post-socialist countries, including Serbia, middle class formation is, and has been, associated with the in-country economic development within the concept of liberal reforms, lionized in the early 1990s. However, Rose (1997) argues that the result of these liberalizing reforms was not the formation of the middle class in itself, but its erosion. Rose (1997) further explains that in an attempt to realize middle-class development as a structure of society in transition, its formation is associated with the exercise of private property rights and entrepreneurship, which both arguably allow earning of disposable income. However, the latter can only be implemented to current conditions provided in-country resources to support entrepreneurship are optimized, and alternative small business are developed.

Serbia's middle class lacks the economic features enjoyed by their equivalents in established capitalist economies. That is, Serbia's middle class requires economic freedom to exercise its own socioeconomic reforms, creating upward mobility, conducive to innovation/entrepreneurship. In order to achieve the appropriate socioeconomic structure, policy making should address the immobility and stagnation of the lower society's layer. In the process of transformation and post transformation, ensuring the necessary legal framework of enforcing property rights and capital flight fosters the favorable conditions of economic growth and social mobility. In fact, Staniszkiz (2007) argues that Serbia remains a country in transition, not yet relevant nor exposed to the challenges and opportunities of economic modernization. Serbia's middle class prospects of quantitative and qualitative development influence creating favorable conditions conducive to the realization of its economic interests. Thereafter, the interest in reproducing social stature based on the levels of education, health and income along with active participation in the public realm is to significantly increase social capital, and to effectively use all forms of ownership suitable to produce innovation, incubate entrepreneurship and to attract investment (Staniszkiz, 2007).

CHAPTER 5:
Middle Class: Axis of Centrality

MIDDLE CLASS: CRITICALITY

The development of the middle class has been a pertinent challenge in every country's economic policy since the industrial revolution era. This tier controls most countries' economies because the middle class forms the engine of consumption (Geithman, 1974). According to research by Lu (2005), approximately 2 billion people control the world economy with a spending capacity of over $69 trillion annually. The figure is expected to rise in the next decade as more economies continue to transform peoples' standards of living. Most huge spenders form a lasting market for companies' products, and also play an influential role in shaping countries' politics. Additionally, multinational companies (MNCs) have been forced to keep up with the increased demand of commodities by ensuring that their production of goods and services meets the taste and preferences of the growing middle class. The tier, globally, controls a significant part of the world's trade activities irrespective of a country's economic conditions. However, the middle class seizes to exist only through the implementation of appropriate policies, promoting its prosperity, and also incentivizing a country's economic performance to progress.

Pereira (1962) explains, in his study on the growth of the Brazilian middle class that Brazil experienced tremendous industrial development after the Great Depression of 1929, due to the efforts of the middle class. Brazil, in fact, implemented industrialization growth models, employed in the United States, to shape its economy. Eventually, the growth of the middle class brought about new management concepts of local industries (Pereira, 1962). Similarly, the group supported establishing large corporations that are still influential in offering employment to Brazil's huge population. Despite the benefits of embracing the middle class, De Lima and Hirst (2006) argue that the country should make solid political and economic decisions, which can further contribute to developing the entirety of Brazil's society.

In addition to Pereira (1962), Camfield (2004) also introduces the class theory to explain concepts about the rise of the middle class in society. In his view, analyzing the composition of a class is essential in studying how the division of labor contributes to developing capitalist production conditions. The class theory supports a procedural set-up where workers can form relations that enable them to discover their potential in managing the growth of an organization and the status of the economy. Camfield's (2004) theory emphasizes that the development of working-class societies is crucial for forming capitalistic communities in which people can undertake any activity they deem necessary to transform their livelihood.

POLITICAL STRUCTURE

Additionally, capitalistic societies have a major impact on the political structure of a country, since class developments are nurtured by leaders who can translate people's needs into economic benefits. In support of Camfield's (2004) study about the development of classes in society, Reay (2005) concurrently describes developments as an outcome of people's psychic responses to the desire to lead a better life. He further explains that the formation of classes is a dynamic transition, which is normally achieved by meeting needs that are associated with particular developments in society. However, Breen and Rottman (1995) argue that the formation of social classes may lead to inequality, because some groups of people are likely to demand more attention than other classes during the process of resource-allocation, carried out by the government. In fact, Breen and Rottman (1995) indicate that class development should not be supported in society because it is reprehensible.

While a number of scholars argue against the class theory, research by King, Nguyen and Minh (2008) studying the growth of the middle class in Vietnam, in relationship to identity and change, underlines how education and the emergence of the private sector have played an influential role in the development of Vietnam's middle class. King et al (2008) argue that a society can be empowered to improve the living standards of individuals by embracing education and cultivating its human capital. The community, hereafter, attracts private sector investments and partnerships whose projects contribute to the growth of the middle class in a country. In fact, the expansion of Vietnam's middle class is said to have increased the level of satisfaction in the country because many of its citizens can afford life's most important needs. Similarly, the transformation has played a major role in shaping the nation's politics since Vietnamese are interested in electing leaders who promise to mobilize public resources for social development instead of personal gains (King et al, 2008).

Equally, Easterly (2001) describes how the middle class is influential in steering a country's economic growth. As his study examines, ethnic divisions are rare in a society that distributes resources among middle- and low-income individuals. Equitable resource sharing, in turn, stimulates economic growth, contributes to political stability, and promotes enactment of appropriate commercial policies. Easterly (2001) concludes that countries that have consensus among the middle class are highly developed and have effective economic policies. Therefore, the growth of a united middle class benefits a country in terms of economic growth and political stability. However, Anthias (2001) scrutinizes how this group of society can be a powerful source of negative ethnical fracture, and communal divisions and identities in a country. He argues that class should not be used as a benchmark for resource allocation and assessment of individuals' abilities in society. Instead, the world should view class stratification as a means of enhancing economic development. Focusing on ethnic divisions in society may have a challenging impact on the government's ability to address material inequalities among individuals.

Figure 5.1:

Rising Middle Classes in the Emerging Market Countries (2000 –2013)

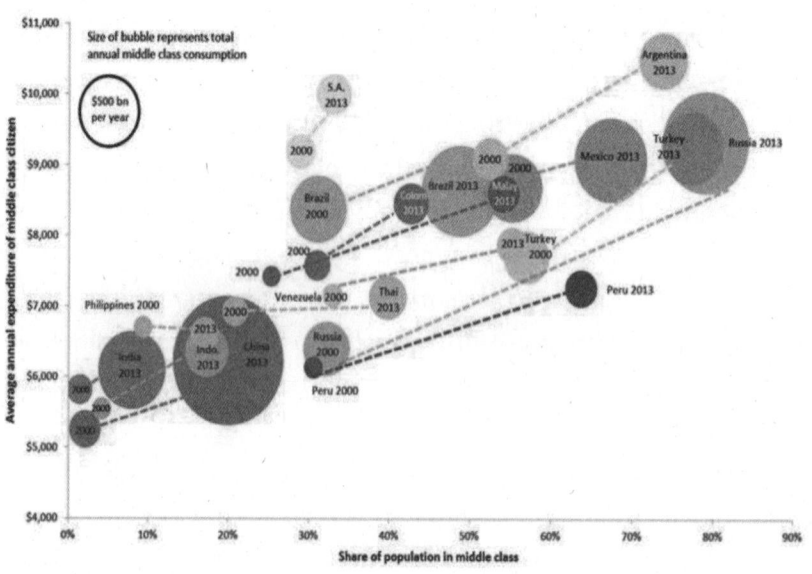

Note: Establishing consistent criteria to define middle classes across emerging market countries is difficult, but this figure utilizes the OECD and Brookings Institution criteria of households with daily expenditures between $10 and $100 per person in purchasing power parity terms in constant 2005 international dollars. While in some countries—particularly Russia—this measure may show an artificially high proportion of the population as being denominated as middle class, it nevertheless captures an important trend.
Source: OECD (2015)

In contrast to Anthias (2001), a study by Koo (1991) on South Korea's middle class correlated to class formation and democratization, points out that the growth of the country's middle class is attributed to the successful, ever-increasing industrialization in South Korea, in particular, and in general the Asian geopolitical bloc. Demand for local skills grows as industries expand; thus, contributing to the percentage increase of middle class citizens in South Korea. In fact, Koo (1991) underlines that the middle class has been influential in transforming the political landscape of South Korea because of the economic power that the group possesses. Most middle-income individuals support initiatives for proper governance and accountability. Additionally, this class growth offers a better ground for enacting superior political and economic principles that significantly contribute to the expansion of its economy. Accordingly, the South Korean experience is a unique case of middle class development since social conflicts and tensions are rarely reported in the country. However, it would have been difficult for South Korea to have the middle class population that it boasts without economic transformation and growth within the Asian region.

In a rather recent study, Lu (2005) stresses how the middle class in a society is a powerful force when implementing strategies that promote democracy. In his study, Lu (2005) describes that a powerful middle class can compel a country's leaders to be accountable for their actions. Therefore, it is only through addressing the in-country economic interests that the middle class would be willing to embrace particular political systems (Malamud, 1998). Countries that do not have an influential middle class are likely to suffer from a lack of participatory political structure, which in turn affects the path of economic development.

MIDDLE CLASS: A FUNCTION OF GROWTH

Klubock (1996) examines the growth impact of Chile's middle class on the country's mining industry. The Chilean society was accustomed to attractive wages that could enable its members to support their families and meet daily expenses. As a result, Klubock (1996) points out, it was inevitable that a tussle would ensue whenever a copper company tried to offer miners meager salaries that could not sustain their livelihood. Mining companies also had limited ability to control workers in fear of reprisals. The emergence of a social class within the mining industry had contributed to its sectorial politics, changing the playing field when workers called for better governance. The main outcome of these actions was the formation of a labor movement which facilitated changes in working-class ideologies in an attempt to improve social and economic benefits for Chileans within the mining industry.

In addition to Klubock's (1996) findings, Berberoglu (2007) argues that development of classes in society steers the political discourse towards societal inequality. That is, class development offers political leaders a reliable framework for understanding the dynamics and contradictions of the capitalist society. Berberoglu (2007) also argues that social classes play a major role in defining how communities relate. For instance, they determine how employers develop an appropriate framework to hire and retain local talent, and also set up the appropriate organizational structures. Wheary (2010) further argues and points out that class analysis plays a central role in determining how society and its members relate and engage with in-country key institutions and organizations. In China, for instance, the middle class have been an influential driving force in the growth of the country's economy. In fact, Li (2008) proposes to include intra- and inter-cultural paradigms when examining the development of class in China.

Similarly, Pressman (2007) concurs that the future of humanity is dependent on the global class struggle, a key determinant in the collapse of poor political structures and governance. In Serbia, the middle class was a powerful force in toppling the country's socialist regimes. The group was a predominant proponent for founding a new political regime, which led to the post-socialist transformation of the country (Lazic & Cvejic, 2011). Additionally, the efforts of Serbia's middle class played a pivotal role in restoring the country's economic performance when it underwent distress. The Serbian middle class still controls a significant part of the country's decisions including electing its leaders, and the country's policy development for social governance.

MIDDLE CLASS: FOSTERING SUSTAINABLE DEVELOPMENT

As global income inequality worsens, the purchasing power along with earned disposable income weakens (Ball, 2001) among the varying social classes, especially the middle class. In fact, Rocha and Miles' (2009) study explains that the shortfall of middle class growth, globally, leads to poor in-country governance. Rocha and Miles (2009) further explain that the production and distribution of goods and services are determined by a relative degree of empowering society's middle class. Additionally, if permitting the wealthy to further amass public resources, the in-country poverty spectrum widens, depleting the socioeconomic structure, while increasing the rate of middle-class decline. Hence, in-country development policies are to mirror a trajectory of social empowerment, which could very much yield societal resilience, provided proper access is warranted to resources and proactive policy implementation, including a financially viable, and sustainability-integrated economic outlook.

Actualizing sustainable development is dependent on the country's ability to provide required entrepreneurial resources, and to also maintain a balanced consumption level of in-country goods and services. Graen (2006) points out that the social-grouping middle class accounts for approximately 70% of product expenditure, created locally. Graen's (2006) study argues that improved economic performance is not only a result of creating goods and services locally, but the latter also depends on the available disposable income across the different social classes. Staniszkis (2007) adds that the growth of the middle class in the context of economic development helps achieve the country's diversification objectives. In fact, Keys (1998) explains in his study on the historical parallels to sustainable development discourse, that the then witnessed surge in private sector profitability is attributed to the low cost of raw materials. The middle class is found to exponentially grow – creating new entrepreneurial ventures, mobilizing human capital and embracing innovation – when access to resources and raw materials is equally granted to all society's members. An economically empowered, and an entrepreneurial middle class compels the in-country political institutions and agencies to allocate adequate resources to key sectors that have a significant impact on raising society's standards of living (Wong & Ying-Yi, 2005).

CHAPTER 6:
Entrepreneurship Exhibiting Socioeconomic Resilience

ENTREPRENEURSHIP: SOCIAL MODELING

As a key, yet advent element of economic development, entrepreneurship in its raw functions determines how society's members identify and seize trading and commercial opportunities. These functions include innovation, risk-taking, accountability and governance – management, yet the latter can only be viable in society where its middle class is granted access to resources. Channeled through entrepreneurship by an evolved middle class, society is able to create new goods and services for its members, boost productivity, and enhance trade benefits in the long term. By recognizing the pivotal role of entrepreneurship in society, interest groups and institutions develop the appropriate response mechanisms to ensure that entrepreneurial activities spur both development and growth. Although, arguably, entrepreneurship exemplifies a method of wealth creation, Morris, Davis, and Allen (1994) explain that failure to identify the essential components to drive growth in business activities may cripple its ability to remain viable or rather economically sustainable. Kuratko, Morris, and Schindehutte (2015) further argue that in order to strike the appropriate balance for all the social, economic, and political undertakings, entrepreneurs and business organizations alike have to align their goals to meet society's set objectives. The proper utility of available resources, made accessible by the in-country political order, translates into socioeconomic mobility, conducive for growth in which entrepreneurship becomes contingent upon.

In addition, Tracey, Dacin, and Dacin (2011) point out that entrepreneurship improves the productivity of the private sector, including for business organizations that formerly depended on the in-country political order and its institutions to carry out business activities in society. In fact, Tracey et al (2011) also point out that by understanding the value of entrepreneurship at the individual level, society's members are able to focus on missions that create value and offer solutions to existing problems. Prefixed with 'social,' social entrepreneurship hereafter involves defining a goal that addresses the challenges civil society, political institutions and innovators alike encounter. Thus, social entrepreneurship becomes a nuanced, yet evolutive form of creativity and innovation that enhances society's members' ability to introduce, scale up and deliver services that meet social needs.

As the advent of social mobility within society's class structure, the entrepreneurial class – derived predominantly from the middle class – develops the necessary frameworks to enhance economic growth by effectively using the existing social networks to gain more knowledge, human capital, and other resources. Peredo and Chrisman (2006) explain that social networks are essential in linking entrepreneurs and investors to the appropriate factors that contribute to business expansion. However, Turner (1979) argues that social entrepreneurs tend to ignore economic outcomes of their activities despite the fact they have an impact on business growth. Additionally, despite being an ideal method to pursue the empowerment agenda, Rodrick (1993) explains that social entrepreneurship has not been efficiently developed or modeled. As a result, many societies still depend on the in-country political order to overcome social problems that affect the performance of its economy. Watson (2013) points out that the in-country institutions need to develop appropriate business models as part of a country's growth agenda.

ENTREPRENEURSHIP: SOCIAL CONTEXTUALIZATION

In the study of entrepreneurial conceptual advancement, Zhou (2004) interestingly argues that ethnicity is a major social phenomenon that affects economic growth, especially when growth is a function of risk-taking. Zhou (2004) points out that as social groups exhibit a wide range of entrepreneurial ideals, 'ethnic' entrepreneurship is constructed by subgroup entrepreneurs and regional intermediaries, which are both comprised of those members who trade with society's elite. In fact, Zhou (2004) further argues that ethnic entrepreneurship within the context of variant social grouping characterizes a policy framework in which society can develop its members, namely those marginalized members. Yet, entrepreneurial reinvestment thereafter becomes the key challenge to a dynamic, socially diverse middle class.

Equally, 'enclave' entrepreneurship conceptualizes those society's members held together by co-ethnicity and social structures. In its historical context, those members often owned and managed entrepreneurial activities in immigrant neighborhoods, occupied by low socioeconomic classes. Klyver and Schenkel (2013) explain that today's socioeconomic conditions are very much different, since ethnic enclaves have evolved into multicultural neighborhoods as affluent communities continue to transform into middle-class suburbs. Enclave entrepreneurship has led to the emergence of a racial or ethnic group that does not necessarily rely on the available resources or clustering of its community's members to conduct business operations. Instead, this social subgroup deals with intermediaries to carry out entrepreneurial activities. Raluca (2013) points out that these activities create employment opportunities for co-ethnic society's members. Enclave entrepreneurship solidifies in its transactional carryout social co-existence and cultural convenience.

COMMUNITY-BASED ENTERPRISES

In practice, social entrepreneurship procreates community-based enterprises (CBEs). Peredo and Chrisman (2006) explain that these enterprises are established owing to the dynamic interaction of society's members: they serve both the entrepreneurs and the community with the aim of improving people's living standards. CBEs extend support to the in-country institutions helping to create and manage new ventures, often embedded in the existing development structures. Additionally, CBEs closely mirror and follow sustainable development ideals, necessary for the long-term socioeconomic growth. In fact, according to Lepoutre, Justo, Terjesen, and Bosma (2013), societies that invest in creating CBEs and in-country institutions that develop these CBE build a better strategy for fostering innovation, creativity and entrepreneurialism.

In CBEs, the community acts as both the enterprise and the entrepreneur. This approach attempts to capture the key social issues and challenges depriving society from development or prosperity. In contrast to conventional business models, formed on the basis of mere profit maximization, CBEs create socially essential frameworks of mitigating social ills. CBEs leverage the community to meet the needs of society, achieving its social gains. Although traditionally business organizations are confined with conventional models of generating wealth and profit, CBEs give entrepreneurship an expanded definition and a new dimension beyond the orthodoxy of profit making; that is, CBEs can employ new business models and recreate organizational structures to help achieve society's social development goals. Rocha (2004) describes CBEs as a critical platform: political institutions can develop the correct response mechanisms to challenges that arise on account of varying cultural and social factors. Rocha (2004) argues that properly developed CBEs become a determinant growth factor and a contributory element in a country's economy. However, Sørensen, and Sharkey (2014) argue that social gains become undermined when CBEs are passive and purely charitable, lacking business fundamentals. In places where the communities' development frameworks are poorly designed to promote entrepreneurial goals, the conventional approach to entrepreneurship, however, may likely yield negligible results, inconsistent with society's expectations (Sørensen & Sharkey, 2014).

ENTREPRENEURSHIP: SOCIAL CONDITIONING

In its theoretical form, entrepreneurship can thrive in a variety of social, economic, and cultural settings irrespective of the number of disposable resources. However, Zhou (2004) points out that a lack of social mobility in society impedes entrepreneurial success. The rigidity or lucidity of social structures in society may either spur or hinder entrepreneurial development. For instance, reduced social mobility implies that the existing market has a significant population that can boost the level of economic activities (Zhou, 2004). Although entrepreneurs can identify the existing gap in the supply of goods and services, developing suitable mechanisms to meet people's needs continues to be a key challenge.

Additionally, economic crises that are mostly caused by minimal trade activities have been found to act as catalysts for venture creation. According to Evans (1982), learning survival strategies is inevitable in periods of financial difficulty. Since people rely on employment as the main source of income, economic challenges often affect them as employers reduce wages or make them redundant. Thriving during seasons of reduced economic productivity requires people to leverage entrepreneurial opportunities that lead to improved financial conditions. Therefore, entrepreneurship is not necessarily an activity that succeeds in periods of abundance; yet, instead, it thrives in all seasons, as long as the appropriate measures for people to conduct business activities appropriately and conveniently are put in place.

In fact, a politically stable society is able to provide its members with essential services that can spur entrepreneurship. Better health care, security, infrastructure, and improved basic income are a few of the prerequisites for successful entrepreneurship. Thornton (1999) explains that the benefits that a community stands to gain by pursuing a development agenda are determined by the level of satisfaction that society's members derive from the provided resources. However, in-country institutions are constantly challenged by energy supply, quality education and income distribution. Hitt, Ireland, Sirmon, and Trahms (2011) argue that although people's standards of living do not inherently reflect the degree of attractiveness for in-country investment, building a stable market for goods and services to be produced and consumed is the cornerstone to further expand entrepreneurship, creating value for society as a whole. Nevertheless, economic analysis may suggest reinvestment of most needed services in low entrepreneurial communities in order to spur growth (Kalantaridis, Lbrianidis, & Vassilev, 2007). Similarly, societies that focus on continued innovation and on effectively leveraging individual member's creativity and innovation to come up with new products or breakthroughs, are likely to exhibit success and resilience to socioeconomic challenges.

ENTREPRENEURSHIP: SOCIAL CAPITAL

Social capital remains an essential ingredient to in-country economic development objectives. According to Carlsson,

Braunerhjelm, McKelvey, Olofsson, Persson and Ylinenpää (2013), entrepreneurship thrives in areas where the in-country leadership develops successive social relations that help in the creation of an environment, which enables and eases business innovativeness and creativity. As Dacin, Dacin, and Matear (2010) explain, the local community is the greatest source of capital for any entrepreneur in which investors can establish strong relationships leading to develop trust and cooperation between and among entrepreneurs, investors and society at large.

Additionally, extensive social relationships further advance the creation of reliable networks that accelerate the ability of the local community and society alike to raise capital. The success of entrepreneurship can be derived from the coordination of its social resources. Tracey et al (2011) argue that a number of local communities not only provide the social resources that promote development, but they also encourage potential investors to focus on business functions that benefit society. However, Sekhar (2005) cautions that relying on social capital to stimulate economic development in society lowers a business organization's ability to execute its functions effectively. As Sekhar (2005) further argues, if the available capital does not meet the expectations of entrepreneurs, the likelihood that investments may collapse or even fail to start is relatively high. Hence, there exists the need to seek other forms of resources required for development, rather than depending entirely on social networks for capital. In fact, Runst (2013) points out that transparency in providing adequate information to entrepreneurs positively impacts the degree of social networking needed. The extent to which in-country institutions and society offer support to investors and entrepreneurs plays a significant role in ensuring that social capital leads to business success.

To achieve the desired entrepreneurial objectives, encouraging society's members to act jointly to produce goods and services becomes paramount when capitalizing on the existing social resources. Gedajlovic, Honig, Moore, Payne, and Wright (2013) explain that since a community refers to a group of people who do not necessarily share the same goals, but who share the same geographical proximity and who have common values and beliefs, reorienting entrepreneurial development to account for the intra-social setting helps in creating a more viable structure for entrepreneurship and investment to thrive. Because of the key role of society in the agenda of development, Frederick and Monsen (2011) advise that in-country institutions should introduce sustainability measures in which business organizations are required to account for society's social gains, allowing for a more inclusive growth outcome – thus, valuing society enriches businesses.

SOCIAL ENTREPRENEURSHIP: SHORTCOMINGS

Social entrepreneurship faces a number of structural challenges that inhibit its further development. According to Levie and Autio (2008), CBEs require caliber expertise to have an impact on the local community. While many CBEs can be managed by local community's members who possess the essential skills and knowledge, the in-country institutions are a critical body in determining and putting into effect the necessary policies for economic growth. In fact, the lack of in-country governmental supervision or oversight of entrepreneurial projects indicates that society's members suffer from consultatory shortcomings – a lack of advice and guidance, on the best practices to managing business organizations. According to Pinillos and Reyes (2011), the technical know-how available in the community can help to implement growth plans, and could remain sustainable in episodes of financial crises.

Additionally, the lack of in-country institutions' and governmental agencies' involvement in socially entrepreneurial projects may limit the capacity of growth to those marginalized communities. Meeting the economic needs of society requires expansive governmental support in the form of financial grants and subsidized loans, permitting entrepreneurship to grow – as depicted in Figure 6.1, the social value created in rethinking the conventional business strategy becomes a function of growth. The absence of a clear entrepreneurial direction weakens social mobility and hinders socioeconomic development, reducing the pace of growth. Estrin, Mickiewicz, and Stephan (2013) point out that low-income society's members are the ones to suffer most in the failure of delivering goods and services. Inadequate resource provision may even minimize the value of entrepreneurial activities if confronted with poor access to social goods. Thomas and Mueller (2000) argue that the development agenda becomes a permanent challenge when capital-intensive projects are left in the hands of a few of society's members.

Figure 6.1:

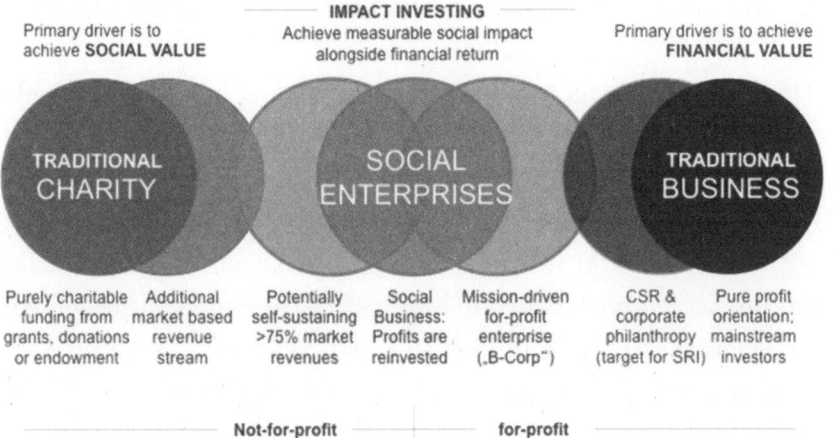

THE BUSINESS MODEL SPECTRUM REVISITED

Despite the central role of the in-country institutions and agencies in the quest of development and growth, advocates of free market ideology endorse autonomy and voluntary exchanges that can exist within exploitative conditions of capitalism. Bielefeld (2009) explains that those who work in social entrepreneurship settings develop appropriate models to improve the environment for investments and better business performance even without the in-country intervention. Those social entrepreneurship leaders are able to maximize productivity, not only for the benefit of their organizations, but also to enhance the living standards of others in society. When provided with adequate resources and the freedom to operate, entrepreneurs – including and especially social ones – are able contribute to the stability of society at large.

SOCIAL ENTREPRENEURSHIP: RETHINKING

The demand for goods and services is rising as society's needs continue to transform socially, politically and economically. Today's entrepreneurial activities are more innovative, creative and socially-driven than past business operations. Entrepreneurship encourages creativity-induced growth that can align profit making with social gains. In fact, entrepreneurship becomes instrumental in the agenda of development if socially inclusive and conducive. An economic policy alone is ill-prepared to combat socioeconomic challenges, yet, prefixed social entrepreneurship marries conventional business ideals to transform society. If envisaged, social entrepreneurship centers the axis of sustainability and social capital when the discourse of development is heightened.

CHAPTER 7:
Limitations: Rethinking Class Analysis – Middle-Class Utility

RETHINKING

The utility of the middle class has long captivated socioeconomic analyses as a societal guarantor of political and economic stability. Often middle class utility carries developmental hopes of an innovative economy, an interactive service industry, and a dynamic market orientation, conceptualized within contemporary capitalist society. In fact, the rise of the middle class as a thriving social grouping in its societal socioeconomic structure of economically developed countries is owing to rather endowed egalitarian, participatory values, and to creativity and innovation-induced in-country policies. In its historical context, the emergence of the middle class in many capitalist societies has been uneven and unparalleled: that is, the sociopolitical peculiarities of the then economic realities have either aided or born the desired growth. However, linear class analysis may not fully nor adequately respond to the issues of economic development without accounting for society's sub-social challenges and cultural nuances.

RETHINKING MIDDLE CLASS UTILITY: CONTEMPORARY RESEARCH

Contemporary research on middle class growth within its economic reality revolves around the contradiction between the knowledge of today's economic requirements and the prerequisites of economic modernization. The latter focuses on three key economic conditions: improving private-sector productivity, the creation of new and modern jobs, and the development of innovative economic – business – activity; yet, the former scrutinizes the lack of socioeconomic knowledge, of constructive in-country policies, and the absence of the socioeconomic-inclusion means to develop a thriving middle class. In fact, contemporary research lionizes middle class development as a pillar of society's capitalistic economic comprehension. However, concurrently, on several accounts, in-depth socioeconomic research regards the middle class as a nominal function of growth in order to understand the necessity and reality of the very existence of potential conflicts between social classes and socioeconomic structures in society (Gimenez, 2001). In these case studies, the middle class becomes a dependent economic variable of average, upper and lower classes, equated with socioeconomic actions.

Milios (2000) argues that contemporary research's interest in the phenomenon of middle class, and its correlation to pure economic prerequisites, arose from the historical study of social marginalization and social inequality in society. As Milios (2000) points out, appearing in the Renaissance era, social inequality has perpetuated and lingered into modern times. Class struggle has received its justification in the works of Karl Marx, incepting the study of middle class on a variety of social and cultural paradigms (Gimenez, 2001). In fact, Milios (2000) further argues that the needed conditions to create the social grouping of the middle class have to meet the global economic conditions' criteria of development, policy reform and growth.

Notwithstanding, Barbalet (1986) argues that social inequality is widely present in today's modern societies. Barbalet (1986) points out that social inequality leads to the emergence of two extreme categories of class grouping which influence how social power impacts societal changes and transformations; namely, the lower stratum of society – the poor and the working class vis-à-vis the highest, richest class. Middle class hereafter becomes an arbitrary social stratum of constant change.

A TREND OF DECLINE

As capitalistic social stratification intensifies, Pressman (2007) argues that the middle class examined in the process of post-industrial economic structure is in decline, especially if the country's economy is not associated nor is it creating added-value industries. In fact, Credit Suisse's Global Wealth Report 2014 depicts a relative decline of the median middle class wealth of key developed economies. As illustrated in Figure 7.1, the US median middle class wealth lags behind much of the world's developed economies. In 21st position, its middle class wealth is less than one-quarter of Australia's for the year of 2014.

Figure 7.1:

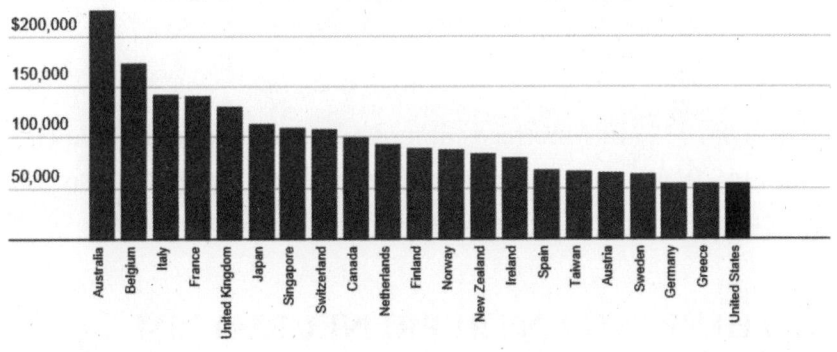

Source: Research Institute Thought leadership from Credit Suisse Research and the world's foremost experts. (2014). Global Wealth Databook 2014. Retrieved on 07 May 2015 from: http://economics.uwo.ca/people/davies_docs/credit-suisse-global-wealth-report-2014.pdf

Additionally, Credit Suisse's Global Wealth Report 2014 explains that American middle class identity is disappearing despite its advanced economic structure. In fact, as represented in Figure 7.2, Pew Research Center's 2014 Report points out that surveyed everyday Americans self-identifying as 'middle class' have significantly decreased in recent years, while the lower-middle-class stratum has increased, suggesting an economic security squeeze out.

Figure 7.2:

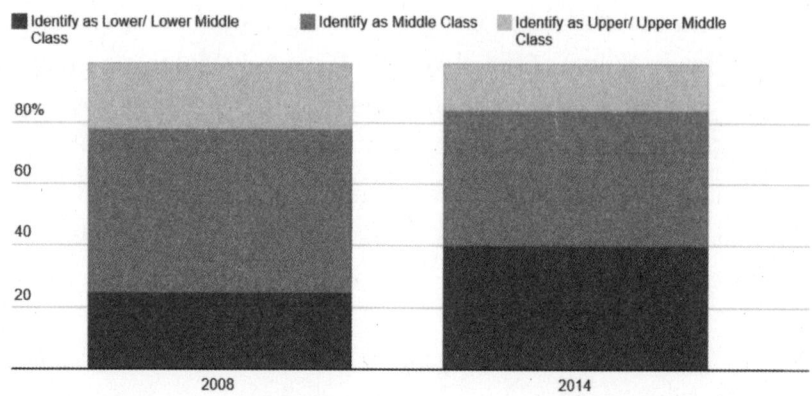

Source: Fact tank from Pew Research Center Report. (2014). Pew Research Center 2014. Retrieved on 08 July 2015 from: http://www.people-press.org/files/legacy-pdf/1-23-14%20 Poverty_Inequality%20Release.pdf

In 2008, 53% of Americans described themselves as middle class, while in 2014, six years later, after the global financial crisis, that percentage consisting of the American middle class dropped to 44%.

RETHINKING ENTREPRENEURIALISM

An indication of economic development is society's members' attitude towards entrepreneurship. In its socioeconomic structure, entrepreneurship allows society to improve its well-being and livelihood by the introduction and consumption of goods and services. In fact, entrepreneurship is dependent on the accessibility of resources including human capital – a key factor much needed to expand the growth of a thriving middle class. In his study of capital transactions across regions and borders, Rodrick (2007) argues that certain regional communities or specific societies that value developing new – potentially creative – ventures realize economic success faster compared to those that depend on the process of importing goods and services. Irrespective of society's attitude towards entrepreneurship, Rodrick (2007) further argues that an in-country governance system shapes the economic structure, required to incubate entrepreneurs, and also influences determining the propensity of entrepreneurial success. Additionally, the in-country political institutions and interest groups play a technocratic role of devising favorable policies to encourage the growth and expansion of the middle class by accessing resources, property rights, financial and human capital. An entrepreneurial middle class is likely to start new ventures, develop and run small and medium enterprises in a specific societal setting or across regions. Importantly, the stability of the governance and policy framework along with the viability of the socioeconomic structure determines the ability of society to succeed in fostering its entrepreneurial middle class, its SMEs, and its development trajectory.

SMEs account for the rapid growth of most economies worldwide, and are predominantly owned by the middle class, comprising of high disposable income and of aptitude to investment (O'Hara, 2000). If fair distribution of resources is ensured, SMEs help in developing the much-needed economic growth, creating employment opportunities, expanding purchasing power, promoting investment and encouraging policy rethinking. Earley's (2006) study reveals that on several accounts, governments rely on the success of SMEs to collect more revenue, translated into a form of taxes. SMEs' expansion in remote areas tasks and supports the in-country governmental agencies to commission subordinating projects such as the construction of roads, access to vendors and facilities, lodging and commercial activity development. In essence, the development of SMEs becomes contributory to an economic policy aimed at alleviating the living standards of society's members in rural areas.

SOCIAL MOBILITY: UPWARD, DOWNWARD OR STAGNANT

Despite its socioeconomic orientation, the middle class remains a conducive societal structure of the high social mobility, both upward and downward, especially when influenced by social marginalization. In essence, social mobility plays a critical role in realizing the country's economic conditions, a rather intuitive trajectory for growth. However, Naude (2010) argues that upward social mobility is relatively weaker in the upper layers of the middle class than those in the lower ones. Naude (2010) further argues that the upper middle class has its own birth rite of passage – only those society's members born into the upper middle class can cease to exist within the upper middle class. Despite the latter, factors to socioeconomic ascension includes economic capacities and capital: that is, the ability to live in contemporary capitalistic market conditions of increased competition, expanded individual freedom, nonconformity of resources, as well as the disparity of caliber. Although the middle class does indeed serve as a social ladder of upward mobility, internalized societal conditions and external economic and political realities shape and grant access to that social ladder.

In fact, socioeconomic research has no unequivocal or common position on the necessity and resolutions to address social mobility vis-à-vis social inequality. On several accounts, socioeconomic research considers the unequal distribution of social goods to serve as a tool for solving society's major problems. Accordingly, there exists an opportunity to reward each member of society depending on his or her own merits (Berberoglu, 1999). The latter is based on a functionalist theory of social inequality, yet there is also a theory of conflict that overlays social inequality. According to Berberoglu (1999), social inequality is the mechanism of human exploitation, and is associated with the struggle for values and scarce resources. Therefore, obtaining the possibility to comparatively consume these resources in greater amounts, leads to social inequality, and does not meet the requirements of social equality and justice (Berberoglu, 1999). However, the continued relevance of the middle class in the discourse of social inequality and social mobility centers on the qualitative characteristics of a capitalist society, featuring a balanced social orientation and creativity/innovation bearing.

If properly developed, the middle class can serve as a socioeconomic platform of in-country growth, and social mobility hereafter becomes a vital element in the economic conditions of the country's long-term development. Enhanced intra-middle class mobility, ascending from lower to middle to upper layers of the middle class, bears a societal economic consciousness, and may evidently require the in-country leadership – political institutions and civil societies, to edify entrepreneurialism, creativity and innovation; and to also grant equal access to recourses and public goods. The middle class carries on transformative values needed in today's market conditions of financial literacy, entrepreneurship, social capital and growth.

CHAPTER 8:
Considerations & Conclusions

SOCIAL CLASSES: SOCIETAL HETEROGENEITY

As social classes evolve and become complex, the economic structures condition the social and political orders. The middle class then orchestrates the success or stability of these orders in the construction of a capitalist society. The middle class possesses a complex and heterogeneous character, evident in developed economies from the time when the social division of society became necessary, and when the creation of a new socioeconomic structure appeared. The middle class performs, primarily, social and economic functions, and acts as a socioeconomic guarantor of the progressive development in society. Importantly, the middle class increases the upward social mobility trend of the ascension from one social layer to another.

As characterized by complexity yet heterogeneity, the middle class phenomenon became widespread during the industrial and post-industrial stages of social development. However, the middle class can also be defined as a unified socially-integral grouping, whose socioeconomic structures share common characteristics in a system of dominance: i.e., education, income, entrepreneurship... etc. The formation of the middle class contributes to the development of economic spectrums, as well as to particular political and socioeconomic activities of the in-country governance direction. In fact, society's division of being middle class is the result of social construction; namely, the advent of analysis and interpretation of economic and social conditions, which the latter influences human existence and society. Hence, these analytical constructions may vary, creating methodological differences.

SOCIETAL CONVICTIONS: CULTURAL DETERMINANTS

As culture is inextricably interwoven with socioeconomic development and growth, cultural values deeply influence the course and rate of economic growth and development. Accordingly, collectivism as a cultural value is seen as repugnant to economic growth and development as the developed West attempts to universalize the value of individualism. That is, those cultures endeavoring individualism promote economic freedom and thus material progress. However, as Ntibagirirwa (2009) argues, although individualism and rational reasoning are not the sole contributory values that accelerate economic growth, cultural values and belief systems move akin and along the path of creating economic development.

In fact, cultural values have an incredible impact on economic development. That is, social capital has a massive influence on transaction costs. Cultures with a well-established social capital have reduced transaction costs, which in turn induces growth. A good example is the Confucian culture, mostly found in East Asia. Lertzman and Vredenburg (2005), and Li (2006) claim that the Confucian culture significantly contributed to the record Asian growth experienced in the 1970s. In the context of Korea's culture, Ntibagiriwa (2009) argues that the socioeconomic development is largely influenced with how formal and informal institutions operate. Culture impacts the operation of formal and informal institutions, and consequently influences economic development. Additionally, Jay and Morad (2002) underline that an increasingly huge number of scholars, including Max Weber, have argued that the difference in economic growth rates in East Asia and the Western developed world stems from the differences in cultural values. As I argued and explained; self-interest, individualistic ethos and social capital promote economic development, and cultivating these values present a cultural strength that enables and ignites economic development. The latter defines those values in a culture that is learned and can be altered with ease.

CULTURALLY CONTRIBUTORY FACTORS: EMPOWERING SUSTAINABILITY

As analyzed, culture defines the collective, societal, thinking process and the behavioral attitudes of society's members in a specific setting. If contextualized in the discourse of development, a society's culture determines the engageability of its members, as well as the pace of economic growth – hence, the collective thinking venture of creativity, novelty and innovation translate into entrepreneurial functions, provided resources are accessed correctly. In fact, Sanwal (2015) argues that culture influences the velocity of knowledge gathering, acquisition and retention, contributory to society's entrepreneurship and innovation; that is, culture bears the indispensable knowledge that accelerates economic development and growth.

Importantly, as Hofstede's six cultural dimensions conduce the comprehension of social specificities along with the utility of managing culture across varying societies, creativity-induced growth, power distribution, hierarchical maneuvering and objectivity become salient in the trajectory of development, especially in a developmental path of viability and sustainability. Among Hofstede's six cultural dimensions, the four main and primary contributory paradigms include individualism, uncertainty avoidance, masculinity, and power distance.

Power Distance

Power distance is critical in identifying how society's members belonging to higher social classes influence the behaviors of those members in lower social classes. As examined, the power distance paradigm implies that a society with a high level of power distance is less likely to accept the introduction and consumption of differing goods and services. In contrast, the impact of power distance is diminutive in a society where the majority of its members belong to the middle class. Hence, the social grouping middle class encourages the acceptance of creativity and innovations across the spectrum of society.

Individualism-Collectivism

Individualism-Collectivism refers to the extent to which members of society cherish relational ideals, values and objectivity. The latter also describes the degree to which society's members, especially those within the middle-class grouping, can make decisions without the influence of others – exercising agency and voice. Many different societies embrace the process of collective decision-making, while others call for independent thinking as a mode of fostering innovation and development (Greif, 1994).

Masculinity – Femininity

Masculinity-femininity gauges how societies that recognize this dimension deal with the values of assertion and performance.

Uncertainty Avoidance

Uncertainty avoidance is associated with the employment of absolute rules in society that members should adhere to in lieu of opting to adapt to tomorrow's nuances.

When Hofstede's cultural lens is deployed, the middle class becomes absorptive of innovation, creativity and entrepreneurship in a lower power distance and uncertainty avoidance cultural setting. These cultural determinants are thereafter conducive to development, and as sustainability cherishes collective actions and embraces affirmative goals, the middle class becomes the incubator of sustainable development: the champion of entrepreneurialism.

As society's cultural values may contribute or limit its ability to remain innovative, cultural determinants classify the actions that society's members take to overcome risks while seizing available opportunities to improve their well-being. On several accounts, Jay and Morad (2002) argue that China's and Japan's socio-cultural specificity has played a key role in developing their middle class and maintaining the growth of their respective economies. Following the rise of Japan's middle class, the country has been able to encourage innovation across different sectors of its economy. Japan's education sector plays a leading role in supporting research and development; thereby, empowering the Japanese society to assess the achievability of its innovations (Ntibagirirwa, 2009). China's diverse cultural setting is also a critical factor, contributing to its rapid development. For instance, the country's traditions enhance the diffusion rate of technology and other modern tools for industrial production. Thus, a culture that allows a majority of its society's members to be innovative is likely to realize socially-conscious sustainable development.

RE-ENGINEERING MIDDLE CLASS: SUSTAINABLE DEVELOPMENT POLICIES

As the growth of the middle class in society contributes to the in-country policy ability to develop its economy, economic growth associated with the middle class often involves cultural determinants, especially in middle-class purchasing power and in its consumption of goods and services. Although Rodrick (2010) defines the middle class as a category of social grouping whose percentile consumption ranges between 20 and 80 – the median per capita ranges at 0.75 and 1.25, cultural determinants of economic growth bearing a thriving middle class centralizes the socioeconomic necessity of class distribution. Beyond the economic metrics, in the utility of Hofstede's six cultural dimensions, uncertainty avoidance becomes contributory to, and has a correlative effect on economic growth. In fact, amidst the pleas to maintain a thriving middle class, the country's governance lacks the appropriate policy language for development, and society lacks the cultural comprehension of its social classes. To remain economically viable and socially stable, the development discourse takes a nuanced policy route, a trajectory towards sustainability and sustainable development.

Sustainable development, in essence, refers to the ability of society to meet today's needs and its interests of the present without jeopardizing the ability of future society's members to manage their own necessities. While recognizing the goals of sustainable development, society's culture, its social grouping and socioeconomic structure become hereafter paramount to achieving these goals (Guiso, Sapienza & Zingales, 2004). Hence, the middle class is aligned with the capacity building of sustainable development as the latter provides the social-grouping variation of middle class with agency and voice – access to resources, disposable income, entrepreneurship and time-orientation adaptability. Subsequently, the economic agency and sociopolitical voice of middle class will ensure, if sustainable development policies are introduced, that in-country resources are distributed and accessed in a manner justly satisfying today's society without compromising the economic-growth leverage required in future societies.

SOCIO-CULTURALITY: DEVELOPMENT DISCOURSE

As culture has encircled the discourse of development, and the nuances of the economic growth to contain social stability and sociopolitical resilience contribution to sustainability, the particularity of society is social-class-specific – its development is hereafter socio-culturally-bound. The values and norms that exist are the determinant factors of how social classes in society refute, amend or cope with the changes of the market economy (Guiso, Sapienza, & Zingales, 2006). Cultural differences, diversity or variety thereof influence and affect economic development as the social interplay of culturally-specific values, depicted by Hofstede's six national dimensions, become affluent in society. However, as the discourse of sustainable development – sustainability has grown over the course of the past few years reaching universal heights, transformative power, self-determination, and uncertainty avoidance are namely the cultural values that reside in the domain of socioeconomic structure and that also promote sustainable development.

To reiterate, the development of the middle class gives birth to an innovative economy, an interactive service industry, and a dynamic market orientation. The rise of the middle class as a thriving social grouping in its societal socioeconomic structure of economically developed countries is owing to participatory values, entrepreneurship, and to creativity and innovation-induced in-country policies. However, as linear class analysis may not fully, nor adequately respond to the issues of economic development, accounting for society's sub-social challenges and cultural nuances has a central utility in devising development and growth.

BIBLIOGRAPHY

Ailincă, A. G., & Iordache, F. (2013). Aspects concerning economic and social factors developments - An assessment at the European Union level. *Financial Studies*, *17*(4), 48-55.

Anthias, F. (2001). The concept of 'social division' and theorizing social stratification: Looking at ethnicity and class. *Sociology*, 35(4), 835-854.

Aristotle. (306 B.C). Politics translated by Benjamin Jowett.

Ball, R. (2001). Individualism, collectivism, and economic development. *Annals of the American Academy of Political and Social Science*, *573*, 57-84.

Barbalet,J. (1986). Limitations of Class Theory and the Disappearance of Status: The Problem of the New Middle Class. *Sociology, 20*(4), 557-575.

Barro, R. & McCleary, R. M. (2003). Religion and Economic Growth across Countries. *American Sociological Review*, 68(5), 760-781.

Barr, P., & Glynn, M. A. (2004). Cultural variations in strategic issue interpretation: relating cultural uncertainty avoidance to controllability in discriminating threat and opportunity. *Strategic Management Journal*, *25*(1), 59-67.

Berberoglu, B. (1999). Nationalism, Class Conflict and Social Transformation in the Twentieth Century. *International Review of Modern Sociology*, 29(1), 77-88.

Berberoglu, B. (2007). The centrality of class in contemporary capitalist society. *International Review of Modern Sociology*, 33(1). 49-67.

Bielefeld, W. (2009). Issues in social enterprise and social entrepreneurship. *Journal of Public Affairs, 15*(1), 69-86.

Blanchet, D. (1991). On interpreting observed relationships between population growth and economic growth: A graphical exposition. *Population and Development Review*, *17*(1), 105-114.

Bottero, W. (2004). Class Identities and the Identity of Class. *Sociology*, *38*(5), 985-1003.

Bowles, S. (2008). Endogenous Preferences: The Cultural Consequences of Markets and Other Economic Institutions, *Journal of Economic Literature*, 36(1), 75–111.

Breen, R., & Rottman, D. (1995). Class analysis and Class theory. *Sociology*, 29(3) 453-473.

Camfield, D. (2004). Re-orienting class analysis: Working classes as historical formations. *Science and Society*, 68(4), 421-446.

Carlsson, B., Braunerhjelm, P., McKelvey, M., Olofsson, C., Persson, L., & Ylinenpää, H. (2013). The evolving domain of entrepreneurship research. *Small Business Economics*, *41*(4), 913-930.

Chakraborty, A. (2002). Issues in Social Indicators, Composite Indices and Inequality. *Economic and Political Weekly*, *37*(13), 1199-1202.

Chandra, K., C. (2009). China and India: Convergence in economic growth and social tensions. *Economic and Political Weekly*, *44*(4), 41-53.

Chapman, M. (1996). Preface Social Anthropology, Business Studies, and Cultural Issues. *International Studies of Management & Organization*, *26*(4), 3-29.

Choy, C. L. (1982). Economic growth and social equity in Singapore: A managerial perspective. *Contemporary Southeast Asia*, *4*(2), 184-209.

Chua, H., Wong, A., K., & Shek, D. L. (2010). Social development in Hong Kong: Development issues identified by Social Development Index (SDI). *Social Indicators Research*, *95*(3), 535-551.

Clough, B. S. (1955). Strategic factors in economic growth: A social science view. *Political Science Quarterly*, *70* (1) 19-27.

Coyne, C.J. & Williamson, C. (2009). *Trade Openness and Culture*. London: Mimeo.

Crutchfield, R.D., & Pettinicchio, D. (2009). 'Cultures of Inequality': Ethnicity, Immigration, Social Welfare, and Imprisonment. *Annals of the American Academy of Political and Social Science*, *623*, 134-147.

Dacin, A. P., Dacin, T. M., & Matear, M. (2010). Social

entrepreneurship: Why we don't need a new theory and how we move forward from here. *Academy of Management Perspectives, 1*(3), 38-57.

Dahrendorf, R. (1959). *Class and Class Conflict in Industrial Society.* London: Routledge.

Daskalovic, D. (2015). *SeeNews. The Corporate Wire. Serbia's 2015 GDP seen down 0.5%, to rebound in 2016 – EY.* Retrieved on 02 June 2015 at:http://wire.seenews.com/news/serbias-2015-gdp-seen-down-0-5-to-rebound-in-2016-ey-469550.

De Lima, S., M., & Hirst, M. (2006). Brazil as an intermediate state and regional power: Action, choice, and responsibilities. *International Affairs (Royal Institute of International Affairs), 80*(1) 21-40.

Earley, P. C. (2006). Leading cultural research in the future: a matter of paradigms and taste, *Journal of International Business Studies, 37*(6), 922–931.

Easterly, W. (2001). The middle class consensus and economic development. *Journal of Economic Growth, 6*(4), 317-335.

Eckersley, R. (2009). Population measures of subjective wellbeing: How useful are they? *Social Indicators Research, 94*(1), 1-12.

Eisner, M. (1992). Long-term Fluctuations of economic growth and social destabilization. *Historical Social Research, 17* (64), 70-98.

Ernest & Young. (2014). *EY Global Review.* London: Ernest & Young Global Limited.

Estrin, S., Mickiewicz, T., & Stephan, U. (2013). Entrepreneurship, social capital, and institutions: Social and commercial entrepreneurship across nations. *Entrepreneurship: Theory & Practice, 37*(3), 479-504.

Euwema, M., Wendt, H., & van Emmerik, H. (2007). Leadership styles and group organizational citizenship behavior across cultures. *Journal of Organizational Behavior, 28*(8), 1035-1057.

Evans, P. (1982). Reinventing the bourgeoisie: State entrepreneurship and class formation in dependent capitalist development. *American Journal of Sociology, 88*, S210-S247.

Fedderke, J., & Klitgaard, R. (1998). Economic Growth and Social Indicators: An Exploratory Analysis. *Economic Development and Cultural Change, 46*(3), 455-489.

Fedderke, J. (1997). Political and social dimensions of economic

Growth. *Theoria: A Journal of Social and Political Theory, (89),* 1-42.

Fedderke, J., De Kadt, R., & Luiz, J. (1999). Economic growth and social capital: A critical reflection. *Theory and Society, 28*(5), 709-745.

Frederick, H., & Monsen, E. (2011). New Zealand's perfect storm of entrepreneurship and economic development. *Small Business Economics, 37*(2), 187-204.

Fry, R. & Kochhar, R. (2014). *America's wealth gap between middle-income and upper-income families is widest on record.* Retrieved on 07 May 2015 from: http://www.pewresearch.org/fact-tank/2014/12/17/wealth-gap-upper-middle-income/.

Gedajlovic, E., Honig, B., Moore, C. B., Payne, G. T., & Wright, M. (2013). Social capital and entrepreneurship: A schema and research agenda. *Entrepreneurship: Theory & Practice, 37*(3), 455-478.

Geithman, D. (1974). Middle class growth and economic development in Latin America. *American Journal of Economics and Sociology, 33*(1), 45-58.

Giddens, A. 1984. *The Constitution of Society: Outline of the Theory of Structuration.* Berkeley, University of California Press.

Giddens, A. 1991. *Modernity and Self-Identity: Self and Society in the Late Modern Age,* Stanford, Stanford University Press.

Gimenez, M. (2001). Marxism, and Class, Gender, and Race: Rethinking the Trilogy. *Race, Gender & Class, 8*(2), 23-33.

Graen, G. B. (2006). In the eye of the beholder: Cross-cultural lesson in leadership from project globe: a response viewed from the third culture bonding (TCB) model of cross-cultural leadership. *Academy of Management Perspectives, 20*(4), 95-101.

Greif, A. (1994). Cultural Beliefs and the Organization of Society: A Historical and Theoretical Reflection on Collectivist and Individualist Societies. *Journal of Political Economy.*102 (5), 912-50.

Guiso, L. & Sapienza, P. & Zingales, L. (2004). The Role of Social Capital in Financial Development, *The American Economic Review, 94*(3), pp. 526-556.

Guiso, L., Sapienza, P. & Zingales, L. (2006). Does Culture Affect Economic Outcomes? *Journal of Economic Perspectives, 20*(2), 23-48.

Guveli, A., Need, A., & de Graaf, N.D. (2007). The Rise of 'New'

Social Classes within the Service Class in the Netherlands: Political Orientation of Social and Cultural Specialists and Technocrats between 1970 and 2003. *Acta Sociologica, 50*(2), 129-146.

Hitt, M. A., Ireland, R. D., Sirmon, D. G., & Trahms, C. A. (2011). Strategic entrepreneurship: Creating value for individuals, organizations, and society. *Academy of Management Perspectives, 25*(2), 57-75.

Hofstede, G. (1980). *Culture's Consequences: Comparing Values, Behaviors, Institutions, and Organizations across Nations.* Beverly Hills, CA: Sage Publications.

Hofstede, G. (1983). National Culture Revisited. *Behavior Science Research, 18*(4), 285-305.

Hofstede, G., & Bond, M.H. (1988). The Confucius Connection: From Cultural Roots to Economic Growth. *Organizational Dynamics, 16*(4), 4-21.

Hofstede, G. (1994). The business of international business is culture. *International Business Review, 3*(1), 1-14.

Horowitz, I.L. (1964). *The new sociology: Essays in social science and social theory in honor of C. Wright Mills.* New York: Oxford University Press.

Inkeles, A. (2000). Measuring Social Capital and Its Consequences. *Policy Sciences, 33*(3), 245-268.

Ivanova, I., Arcelus, F., & Srinivasan, G. (1999). An Assessment of the Measurement Properties of the Human Development Index. *Social Indicators Research: An International and Interdisciplinary Journal for Quality-of-Life Measurement, 46*(2), 157-179.

Jay, M., & Morad, M. (2002). Cultural outlooks and the global quest for sustainable environmental management *Geography, 87*(4), 331-335.

Kalantaridis, C., Lbrianidis, L., & Vassilev, I. (2007). Entrepreneurship and institutional change in post-socialist rural areas: Some evidence from Russia and the Ukraine. *Journal for East European Management Studies, 12*(1), 9-34.

Kamdar, S., & Basak, A. (2005). Beyond the Human Developed index: Preliminary note on Deprivation and Inequality. *Economic and Political Weekly, 40*(34), 20-26.

Kanti, R. A. (2008). Measurement of social development: An international comparison. *Social Indicators Research*, *86*(1), 1-46.

Kaufman, P. (2005). Learning to Not Labor: How Working-Class Individuals Construct Middle-Class Identities. *The Sociological Quarterly*, *44*(3), 481 - 504.

Kegley, C., & Blanton, S. (2013). *World Politics: Trend and Transformation, 2014 – 2015*. Boston: Cengage Learning.

Keys, E. (1998). Historical parallels to sustainable development discourse. A review essay. *Revista Geográfica*, *124*, 79-85.

King, V. T., Nguyen, A. P., & Minh, N. H. (2008). Professional middle class youth in post-reform Vietnam: Identity, continuity, and change. *Modern Asian Studies*, 42 (4), 783-813.

Kingston, P.W. (2000). *The Classless Society*. Stanford, CA: Stanford University Press.

Kiuranov, C. (1982). Social Classes and Social Stratification. *International Journal of Sociology*, *12*(3), 1-100.

Klubock, T. M. (1996). Working-class masculinity, middle-class morality, and labor politics in the Chilean copper mines. *Journal of Social History*, 30(2), 435-463.

Klyver, K., & Schenkel, M. T. (2013). From resource access to use: Exploring the impact of resource combinations on nascent entrepreneurship. *Journal of Small Business Management*, *51*(4), 539-556.

Koo, H. (1991). Middle classes, democratization, and class formation: The case of South Korea. *Theory and Society*, 20(4), 485-509.

Kuratko, D., Morris, M., & Schindehutte, M. (2015). Understanding the dynamics of entrepreneurship through framework approaches. *Small Business Economics*, *45*(1), 1-13.

Lanzi, D. & Delbono, F. (2005). A class of human development measures. *Rivista Internazionale di Scienze Sociali*, *113*(4), 537-551.

Lazic, M., & Cvejic, S. (2011). Post-socialist transformation and value changes of the middle class in Serbia. *European Sociological Review*, 27(6) 808–823.

Lepoutre, J., Justo, R., Terjesen, S., & Bosma, N. (2013). Designing a global standardized methodology for measuring social entrepreneurship activity: The Global Entrepreneurship Monitor social entrepreneurship study. *Small Business Economics*, *40*, 693–714.

Lertzman, A. D. & Vredenburg, H. (2005). Indigenous peoples, resource extraction and sustainable development: An ethical approach. *Journal of Business Ethics*, *56*(3), 239-254.

Levie, J., & Autio, E. (2008). A theoretical grounding and test of the GEM model. *Small Business Economics*, *31*(3), 235-263.

Li, H. (2006). The emergence of the Chinese middle class and its implications. *Asian Affairs*, 33(2) 67-83.

Li, M. (2008). Socialism, capitalism, and class struggle: The political economy of modern China. *Economic and Political Weekly*, 43(52), 77-85.

Lind, N. (2004). Values Reflected in the Human Development Index. *Social Indicators Research: An International and Interdisciplinary Journal for Quality-of-Life Measurement*, *66*(3), 283-293.

Lind, N. (2019). A Development of the Human Development Index. *Social Indicators Research: An International and Interdisciplinary Journal for Quality-of-Life Measurement*, *146*(3), 409-423.

Lu, C. (2005). Middle class and democracy: Structural linkage. *International Review of Modern Sociology*, 31(2), 157-178.

Malamud, D. C. (1998). Engineering the middle classes: Class line-drawing in New Deal Hours legislation. *Michigan Law Review*, 96(8), 2212-2321.

Marsh, R.M. (2003). How Important is Social Class Identification in Taiwan? *The Sociological Quarterly*, *44*(1), 37-59.

Marshall, G., & Swift, A. (1993). Social Class and Social Justice. *The British Journal of Sociology*, *44*(2), 187-211.

Marx, K., & Engels, F. (2008). *The Communist manifesto*. London, Pluto Press.

Mazumdar, K. (1996). An analysis of causal flow between social development and economic growth: The Social Development Index. *American Journal of Economics and Sociology*, *55*(3), 361-383.

McBain, D., & Alsamawi, A. (2014). Quantitative accounting for social economic indicators. *Natural Resources Forum*, *38*(3), 193-202.

McSweeney, B. (2002). Hofstede's model of national cultural differences and their consequences: A triumph of faith – a failure of analysis. *Human Relations*, *55*(1), 89-11.

Milios, J. (2000). Social Classes in Classical and Marxist Political Economy. *American Journal of Economics and Sociology, 59*(2), 283-302.

Miller, K. & Madland, D. (2014). *What the New Census Data Show about the Continuing Struggles of the Middle Class.* Retrieved on 07 May 2015 from: https://www.americanprogress.org/issues/economy/news/2014/09/16/97203/what-the-new-census-data-show-about-the-continuing-struggles-of-the-middle-class/.

Mills, C.W. (1951). *White collar: The American middle classes.* New York: Oxford University Press.

Mondale, J.J., & Canache, D. (2004). Knowledge Variables in Cross-National Social Inquiry. *Social Science Quarterly, 85*(3), 539-558.

Morley, S. (1983). *Labor Markets and Inequitable Growth* London: Cambridge University Press.

Morris, M., Davis, D. L., & Allen, J. W. (1994). Fostering corporate entrepreneurship: Cross cultural comparisons of the importance of individualism versus collectivism. *Journal of International Business Studies, 25*(1), 65-89.

Moudatsou, A. & Kyrkilis, D. (2011). FDI and economic growth: Causality for the EU and ASEAN. *Journal of Economic Integration, 26*(3), 554-577.

Naguib, R. & Smucker, J. (2009). When economic growth rhymes with social development: The Malaysia experience. *Journal of Business Ethics, 89*(2), 99-113.

Naude, M. (2010). Entrepreneurship, developing countries, and development economics: New approaches and insights. *Small Business Economics, 34*(1), 1-12.

Nissel, M. (1995). Social Trends and Social Change. *Journal of the Royal Statistical Society. Series A (Statistics in Society), 158*(3), 491-504.

Ntibagiriwa, S. (2009). Cultural Values, Economic Growth and Development. *Journal of Business Ethics, 84*(3), 297-311.

Organization of Economic Cooperation and Development (OECD). (2015). *In It Together: Why Less Inequality Benefits All.* Paris: OECD.

O'Hara, D. (2000). Capitalism and Culture: Bourdieu's Field Theory. *American Studies, 45*(1): 43-53.

Pakulski, J., & Waters, M. (1995). *The Death of Class.* London: SAGE Publications.

Parks, C. D., & Vu, A. D. (1994). Social dilemma behavior of individuals from highly individualist and collectivist cultures. *Journal of Conflict Resolution, 38*(4), 708–718.

Peredo, A., & Chrisman, J. J. (2006). Toward a theory of community based enterprise. *The Academy Management Review, 31*(2), 309-328.

Pereira, B. (1962). The rise of the middle class and middle management in Brazil. *Journal of Inter-American Studies,* 4 (3), 313-326.

Pew Research Center Report. (2014). *Pew Research Center 2014.* Retrieved on 08 July 2015 from: http://www.people-press.org/files/legacy-pdf/1-23-14%20Poverty_Inequality%20Release.pdf.

Pinillos, M., & Reyes, L. (2011). Relationship between individualist-collectivist culture and entrepreneurial activity: evidence from Global Entrepreneurship Monitor data. *Small Business Economics, 37*(1), 23-37.

Platteau, J. (2000). *Institutions, Social Norms, and Economic Development.* Amsterdam: Routledge.

Pradhan, R. P., Mukhopadhyay, B., Gunashekar, A., Samadhan, B., & Pandey, S. (2013). Financial development, social development, and economic growth: The causal nexus in Asia. *Decision (0304-0941), 40*(1/2), 69-83.

Pressman, S. (2007). The decline of the middle class: An international perspective. *Journal of Economic Issues,* 41(1), 181-200.

Raluca, B. M. (2013). Social capital framework and its influence on the entrepreneurial activity. *Annals of the University of Oradea, Economic Science Series, 22*(1), 581-589.

Reay, D. (1998). Rethinking Social Class: Qualitative Perspectives on Class and Gender. *Sociology, 32*(2), 259-275.

Reay, D. (2005). Beyond consciousness? The psychic landscape of social class. *Sociology,* 39 (5), 911-928.

Research Institute Thought leadership from Credit Suisse Research and the world's foremost experts. (2014). *Global Wealth Databook 2014.* Retrieved on 07 May 2015 from: http://economics.uwo.ca/people/davies_docs/credit-suisse-global-wealth-report-2014.pdf.

Rocha, H. O. (2004). Entrepreneurship and development: The role of clusters. *Small Business Economics, 23*(5), 363-400.

Rocha, H. & Miles, R. (2009). A model of collaborative entrepreneurship for a more humanistic management. *Journal of Business Ethics*, *88*(3), 445-462.

Rodrick, D. (1993). The positive economics of policy reform. *The American Economic Review*, *83*(2), 356-361.

Rodrick, D. (2007). *One economy, many recipes: Globalization and economic growth*. Princeton, NJ: Princeton University Press.

Rodrick, D. (2010). Diagnostic before prescription. *Journal of Economic Perspectives*, *24*(3), 33-44.

Rose, F. (1997). Toward a Class-Cultural Theory of Social Movements: Reinterpreting New Social Movements. *Sociological Forum*, *12*(3), 461-494.

Runst, P. (2013). Post-socialist culture and entrepreneurship. *American Journal of Economics and Sociology*, *72*(3), 1-35.

Sanwal, M. (2015). Global sustainable development goals are about the use and distribution, not scarcity of natural resources: will the middle class in the USA, China and India save the climate as its incomes grow? *Climate & Development*, *7*(2), 97-99.

Smallbone, D., Welter, F. (2001). The Distinctiveness of Entrepreneurship in Transition Economies. *Small Business Economics*, *16*(4), 249-262.

Scott, J. (2002). Social Class and Stratification in Late Modernity. *Acta Sociologica*, *45*(1), 23-35.

Sekhar, C. S. C. (2005). Economic growth, social development and interest groups. *Economic and Political Weekly*, *40*(50), 5338-5339.

Slomczynski, K.M., & Janicka, K. (2008). Polarized Social-Class Structure. On the Matthew Effect and Increasing Inequality. *Polish Sociological Review*, *168*, 341-357.

Sørensen, J. & Sharkey, A. (2014). Entrepreneurship as a mobility process. *American Sociological Review*, *79*(2), 328–349.

Staniszkis, J. (2007). Global challenges, culture and development. *Polish Sociological Review*, *159*, 263-281.

Staples, C.L., Schwalbe, M.L., & Gecas, V. (1984). Social Class, Occupational Conditions, and Efficacy-Based Self-Esteem. *Sociological Perspectives*, *27*(1), 85-109.

The Economist Intelligence Unit. (2015). *Country Report: Serbia*. London: The Economist.

Thomas, S. A., & Mueller, S. L. (2000). A case for comparative entrepreneurship: Assessing the relevance of culture. *Journal of International Business Studies*, *31*(2), 287-301.

Thornton, P. H. (1999). The sociology of entrepreneurship. *Annual Review of Sociology*, *25*, 19-46.

Tracey, P., Dacin, T. M., & Dacin, P. A. (2011). Social entrepreneurship: A critique and future directions. *Organization Science*, *22* (5), 1203-1213.

Turner, B. S. (1979). The middle classes and entrepreneurship in capitalist development. *Arab Studies Quarterly*, *1*(2), 113-134.

Watson, T. J. (2013). Entrepreneurship in action: Bringing together the individual, organizational and institutional dimensions of entrepreneurial action. *Entrepreneurship & Regional Development*, *25*(5/6), 404-422.

Weller, C.E., & Logan, A.M. (2009). Measuring Middle Class Economic Security. *Journal of Economic Issues*, *43*(2), 327-336.

Wheary, J. (2010). The global middle class is here: Now what? *World Policy Journal*, *26*(4), 75-83.

Wong, R. Y. & Ying-Yi, H. (2005). Dynamic influences of culture on cooperation in the prisoner's dilemma. *Psychological Science*, *16*(6), 429-434.

Zagler, M. (2009). Economic growth, structural change, and search unemployment. *Journal of Economics*, *96*(1), 63-78.

Zeitlin, M. (1974). Corporate Ownership and Control: The Large Corporation and the Capitalist Class. *American Journal of Sociology*, *79*(5), 1073-1119.

Zhou, M. (2004). Revisiting ethnic entrepreneurship: Convergences, controversies, and conceptual advancements. *International Migration Review*, *38*(3), 1040-1074.